Dedication

For my beautiful niece, Mikayla Rose.

May the universe always be kind to your spectacular soul!

Taming the Anxiety Beast

Taming the Anxiety Beast

Workbook for Teens

H.S. Ritter

Contents

Introduction

"What the caterpillar calls the end of the world, the master calls a butterfly."
— Richard Bach

When I was a teenager, riddled with anxiety, self-doubt, and a general sense of impending doom, I was sure that the only person who felt that way was me. Everyone else seemed to be going about their lives just fine, but I was always freaking out and trying not to let it show. I spent the better part of my life searching for ways to manage, navigate, and hide from my extremely uncomfortable feelings. Most of the time, I avoided my feelings by shutting myself in my room with my nose buried in a book, but that is only because we didn't have social media back then. I would have been sucked into Instagram if that had been an option.

I was trying to hide from the things that scared me,

which was an extremely ineffective strategy given that most of what I was afraid of were just ordinary parts of life. Turns out that a lot of the things that freaked me out were there every single time I had to leave the house. Bees, spiders, dogs, people, and all the other scary problems were just waiting for me to come outside. I needed tools to help me work my way through my fears, but back then, not much was available. As I got older, my fears changed, but my ability to hide from them remained unreliable. I would be afraid I would fail a test, but I would still have to take it. I would be afraid I would drop the ball in P.E., but I would still have to play. I was constantly stressed. I wish I had had this book when I was in school. I would have been able to accomplish so much more.

Anxiety has been around for as long as people have, so, if you are as anxious as I was, you are not only not alone, but you have a lot of company. It is not that I like that everyone else is suffering; I just have to admit that sometimes I like knowing that I am not the only one who is floundering.

In 1985, 18% of teens reported that they "felt overwhelmed by all they had to do." By 2010, that number had risen to 29%. Now jump forward to 2016, and that number was at 41%. That means that by now, close to half of the teens you know have anxiety. Half seems like an awful lot, right? Because it is!

It is not shocking to me that those numbers have been growing since the '80s. There were just a lot fewer things to worry about back then. There are countless reasons why more teens are feeling anxious today than ever before. You have to deal with hormonal changes, peer pressure, sports, parents who regularly annoy you, and dozens of other things, not to mention figuring out what you want to do with your life before you even have a job or have picked a college. And if those things weren't already exhausting enough, when the 2020 pandemic hit, it made things even scarier than they already were. We all had to deal with so many new and uncomfortable things, like virtual school, being away from friends, having more conflicts with our families, and worrying that someone we love would get sick. No wonder you are feeling anxious!

Anxiety takes a major toll on your mental health. It can start to affect your school performance and change how you interact with the people in your life. It can be both sneaky and insidious, sometimes affecting almost every area of your life. A lot of people recognize the impact anxiety has on their lives but feel like they don't have any solutions. It seems really unfair that feeling powerless over your feelings is only going to make you feel more anxious. Whoever came up with that idea needs a talking-to!

When anxiety really gets ramped up, it can feel like everything is coming apart at the seams. You may feel terrified of disappointing your parents, being left out of your friend group, or failing at school. It gets even worse when you feel like there is no one to talk to about what you're going through, so you have to go through it all by yourself.

Introduction

You. Are. Not. Alone.

One of the biggest lies that anxiety tells you is that you are the only one who has ever felt this way. That is definitely not true. I work with people, talking to them all day long, and I hear all about the stress and anxiety they are dealing with. When I see eight clients in a day, most of the time at least half of them are in panic mode. In my opinion, the biggest epidemic out there is the absolute overwhelm so many people are suffering through right now.

It took me over three decades to figure out how to overcome my anxiety. I have read books, talked with experts, and sought professional help. This process taught me a lot and gave me the tools I needed to stop anxiety from controlling me. I don't want you to suffer for as long as I did. In the following pages, I will guide you through all the information you need to understand, take charge of, and move beyond your anxiety. You can do it. I am living proof! That doesn't mean you will never have anxiety again; it simply means that when you do, it won't *own* you! You will be able to fight back and win.

Did you know that Selena Gomez suffered from anxiety? It got so bad that she checked herself into a ninety-day treatment center. She had to take the time to understand what was going on in her mind and learn the tools she needed to regain her peace. It takes a lot of courage to face your inner demons, and it was extremely brave and generous of her to be honest about her struggles. She helped so many people by publicly talking about her experience. She learned the kinds of tools I want you to learn from this book, and you don't even have to be rich and famous to get them!

By completing the exercises included here, you can find ways to manage your stress and anxiety even when faced with difficult situations. This will help you feel more in control of your life and emotions. Imagine how much calmer and more peaceful things would be without the weight of the Anxiety Beast sitting on you every second of every day. Once you learn to tame that annoying monster, you can wake up with a smile on your face instead of with the dread of facing another anxious day. How nice would it be to fall asleep quickly because you're no longer fighting all that tension or battling those spinning thoughts in your brain?

As you grow and learn throughout this book, your friends and family may start to notice a difference. You may hear things like, "You seem really happy lately," or "Wow, you are doing things that used to scare you." Your friends, family, and teachers will be so proud of your growth, and you will be proud of your own progress! You may even inspire people to learn more about these tools for themselves.

Hopefully, you have already realized that you don't have to power your way through difficult feelings and you don't have to suffer from anxiety for the rest of your life. If you do the work now, you can enjoy the bright future ahead of you. Or, better yet, we will do the work together! I will be your guide through this process, showing you each step of the way how you can achieve a life beyond anxiety.

Medical Disclaimer: I am not a medical professional, and this book is not intended to be a substitute for professional medical advice, diagnosis, and treatment. I highly recommend seeing a counselor and/or psychiatrist for additional help as needed.

Trigger Warning: This book contains descriptions of anxiety and discussions around symptoms that may act as triggers for your own anxiety.

Chapter One

Anxiety 101

"Do what you can, with what you've got, where you are."
— Squire Bill Widener

It is pretty rare that I get chased by a lion. Okay, I have never been chased by one, but there have been far too many times when my body acted like that's what was happening. I could barely breathe, I felt like I was about to faint, and my mind just seemed to shut down. Sound familiar? I'll bet there has been a time when you felt the same way. Your heart was beating fast, your thoughts were spinning, and your body was drenched in sweat. Everything felt scary and overwhelming and you just wanted to run and hide.

This is a classic picture of anxiety. Our bodies react

like we're running from fearsome beasts, but in reality, we're not trying to escape from becoming something's dinner. No, for those of us who deal with anxiety, this feeling can be triggered by "normal" things like being in a big crowd, taking a test, or doing something new. Sometimes you may even feel anxious for no particular reason.

When you are struggling with anxiety, it can feel like you are trapped in an endless loop of worry and fear. You feel like your anxiety is in control of your life, which makes you feel even more anxious. You eventually become anxious about your own anxiety!

You can stop the cycle and get your body and mind back to a healthier, happier, more peaceful place. But first, you need to understand what is actually going on in your body when you feel anxious.

It turns out that your brain has a "danger sensor." The amygdala is a small part of the brain that takes control of your whole body at any hint of trouble. According to the amygdala, there are only two possible responses to danger: fight or flight.

These responses were helpful to our ancient ancestors when they faced off against woolly mammoths and saber-toothed tigers. Even today, these responses can be entirely appropriate and work really well when we're faced with truly dangerous situations. The problem is that your amygdala doesn't know the difference between public speaking and being physically attacked.

When your brain issues the same bodily response to life-threatening dangers as it does to talking to that popular kid, it makes things even harder than they already are.

The reason your body goes haywire when you feel anxious is because of the amygdala's misguided attempts to be helpful. It tells your heart to beat faster and your muscles to get tense so you can fight at a moment's notice. It makes you breathe more heavily so that you have enough oxygen to run away. Then it sends the signal for your sweat glands to work overtime to cool you down so you don't overheat as you fight or take flight. This is awesome if you are being mugged, but it's less useful if you are just trying to pass your math test.

Let's just step back for a moment and think about how amazing it is that one little part of your brain can wield that much control over the rest of your body. We may curse how the amygdala makes us feel, but the reality is that we would all be in serious trouble without it. There are some scary situations where our stress response is beneficial, but when raising your hand in class makes you feel like you are being chased by a monster, something needs to change.

Understanding how your body responds to stress is an important step toward overcoming anxiety. It helps to know what is going on and to remind yourself that there is nothing physically wrong with you in those stressful moments, even though it can feel like you are having a heart attack or are about to pass out. The amygdala can be such a drama queen!!

Is It Stress or Anxiety?

I used to get confused between stress and anxiety. An easy way for me to remember the difference is that stress is *external* while anxiety is *internal*. You may get stressed because you just fought with your best friend or you forgot to study for a test. In those cases, there is something going on around you that makes you feel stressed. Anxiety, on the other hand, is an overwhelming *internal* fear that occurs in situations that are not actually threatening.

Stress and anxiety are closely related because stress can trigger anxiety. For example, you may get stressed because you were almost in a car accident, but that stress becomes anxiety when you continue to feel tense and scared even after you realize your car was not hit. If you are getting short of breath and sweaty the next time you back out of the driveway, the stress has passed but the anxiety remains.

Everyone reacts to anxiety a little differently. In fact, there are five main types of anxiety disorders. Read through this list with an open mind and see if one seems familiar to you. Try to remember that you are learning about anxiety so that you can be empowered to enjoy a richer, fuller life. So don't get discouraged if you feel like one of these describes you. I have had every single one of them at one time or another. Think of this as an opportunity to gain clarity about something that has been confusing. That just means you're that much closer to feeling better!

The Five Main Types of Anxiety

1. <u>Generalized Anxiety Disorder:</u> This is the most common kind of anxiety. It basically means that you feel super worried for no particular reason. Your baseline is to generally feel tense and on edge.

2. <u>Panic Disorder:</u> People with this disorder feel totally fine and then have an unexpected burst of extreme fear. They have a strong physical response to anxiety including chest pain, shortness of breath, nausea, abdominal pain, or dizziness. (The good news is that you will not actually die from a panic attack—no matter how scary they are.)

3. <u>Social Anxiety Disorder:</u> If everyday social situations make your amygdala go crazy, you may have social anxiety disorder. This makes you feel really self-conscious and worry that others are always looking at you and judging you. It can make talking to people (even your friends sometimes) or going to a party pretty miserable.

4. <u>Obsessive-Compulsive Disorder (OCD):</u> OCD is sometimes made fun of in the media. We've all seen a germ-obsessed character washing their hands a million times. Basically what's going on is that they have an uncomfortable or unwelcome thought (obsession) that they try to get rid of through a certain repetitive behavior (compulsion).

OCD can show up in several different ways. For example, when I struggled with OCD I couldn't sleep unless I checked to make sure the doors were locked several times in a row and then wedged something under the door.

5. <u>Post-Traumatic Stress Disorder (PTSD)</u>: People with PTSD have been through a terrifying event such as abuse, assault, military combat, an accident, or a natural disaster. When something reminds them of that event, they have flashbacks and their body reacts like they are still in that terrifying place.

If you recognize yourself in these descriptions, you should talk to a professional to get a diagnosis and treatment plan. If you recognize yourself in one of those descriptions or have received a formal anxiety diagnosis, please remember that you are not alone. Anxiety disorders are the most common mental health problem in the United States. There are literally millions of other people who feel the same way. That means that there are also many people who have won the battle against anxiety. You can overcome it too. Knowing which type of anxiety you are dealing with is the first step toward overcoming it!

When Does Anxiety Become a Problem?

Everyone feels stressed or anxious at some point in their lives. So how do you know when your anxiety is getting out of control? Well, think about how much anxiety affects your everyday life. If you volunteer to give a presentation even though you feel nervous about it, then you are in control of your anxiety. But, on the other hand, if you skip class or pretend to be sick so you can stay home on the day of the presentation just so you don't have to do it, then your anxiety is in control of you.

It's normal to feel anxious, but it's not normal to feel like anxiety is taking over your life and limiting what you can do. If you are feeling anxious every day or having intense symptoms of anxiety like panic attacks, then anxiety is definitely a problem. Thankfully, there is a solution.

<u>Anxiety is a problem when you have these kinds of symptoms:</u>

- Recurring fears and worries about routine parts of everyday life
- Irritability and feeling like you get angry at any little thing
- Trouble concentrating because your thoughts are often spinning
- Extreme self-consciousness or sensitivity to criticism
- Withdrawal from social activities
- Avoidance of difficult or new situations
- Chronic stomachaches or headaches
- A drop in grades or refusal to go to school
- Repeated reassurance-seeking
- Sleep problems

- Turning to drugs or alcohol to try to manage your anxiety

So What Is Causing My Anxiety?

Though there is a seemingly endless list of things we can find ourselves being anxious about, there are three major things that most teens worry about: how they are perceived, how they perform in school, and how they look. We will look further into each of these causes below. But beyond that, there are also bigger issues at play like your genetics, who is around you, and what is in your environment. In this section, we will look at each of these causes. Once we understand the causes, then it's easier to find the solutions.

Many people—in fact, almost everybody, not just teenagers—are concerned about how they are perceived by other people. They worry about how they look, whether they are wearing the right clothes, and whether they are saying or doing the right things. This anxiety can make some of them obsess over their appearance and constantly scan their environment to see how everyone is reacting to them. When you are constantly worried about being rejected, you will constantly assess whether or not you are fitting in.

School is another big cause of anxiety. You may be worried that you will bring home a grade that makes your parents mad or that you will miss a catch and let your team down. This kind of pressure can quickly spiral into anxiety about the future, what you will do for a career, or if you will be able to achieve your dreams.

Most teens also worry about their bodies. Everyone has at least one body feature that they wish they could change. No one has a perfect body, but many teens feel the pressure to fit the cultural ideal of perfection. This is especially hard for teens because when you're a teenager, your body is not yet fully formed. It is in the middle of some serious changes outside of your control, and you are not sure how it is all going to turn out. The teen years are not an easy time for you or your body!

Did you know that anxiety may be part of your genetics? That means that if one of your parents has anxiety, you are more likely to have it too. Instead of my mother's blue eyes and beautiful singing voice, I got stuck with my father's flat butt and constant worry. Seems a little unfair, right? Them's the genetic breaks, I suppose. When you have blood relatives who battle anxiety, you are more likely to develop anxiety than people without those genes. Your anxiety might be more than just psychological; it might actually be physical!

In addition to genetics, you can also pick up anxiety if you're around it a lot. You know how people from one area of the world can all have the same accent? That isn't genetic. Over time, their speech patterns gradually conformed to those of the people around them. The same thing can happen with anxiety. If you are around a lot of people with anxiety, you are more likely to be anxious too.

Your environment may also be contributing to your

anxiety. For example, if you live in the Midwest and survive a tornado, then just seeing storm clouds out the window can trigger an anxious response in your body and mind. Other common environmental causes of anxiety may include the death of a loved one, a major illness, abuse, being bullied, or frequent moves, any of which can make you feel more tense.

Finally, it is important to realize that anxiety can look different throughout your life. An anxious child may be scared of the dark or think there are monsters under the bed. Their anxiety is focused on external things. But when they become a teenager, that anxiety turns inward. At that point in life, they are more likely to be worried about themselves, their performance, their body, social acceptance or rejection, and how others see them. This can shift again in adulthood, when an anxious adult starts worrying a lot about their children or their finances.

Don't Believe Everything You Hear

I find it very annoying that there is so much bad information out there about anxiety. People who do not have anxiety or really know anything about it end up spreading false information that can cause a lot of harm. So, I think it's important that you know the truth behind each of these ten terrible myths.

1. Myth: Anxiety in teens is not a big deal.

Truth: Do you remember those big numbers in the introduction? This problem affects so many people!

Anxiety causes major problems in their lives, such as time away from school, physical illness, and increased conflicts with family and friends. Anxiety can cause issues in all areas of life. That is, in fact, a very big deal!

2. Myth: Anxiety disorders in children and teens are rare.

Truth: There are approximately 4.4 million Americans between the ages of three and seventeen who have anxiety disorders. And those are just the diagnosed ones! Many others suffer in silence. This is a big problem, and, unfortunately, it is pretty common. UFO sightings are rare. Anxiety disorders are definitely not.

3. Myth: Anxiety in teens is a result of poor parenting.

Truth: Parenting affects children, but it is not the main or only cause of anxiety. In many families with multiple children, only one child has anxiety. That child likely had a genetic predisposition to be anxious, or they may have lived through a traumatic event that sparked their anxiety. Plenty of wonderful parents have anxious children.

4. Myth: A teen can stop being anxious if they want to.

Truth: Okay, this one really ticks me off! No one wants to be anxious, and anxiety isn't a button that can be turned on or off. Overcoming anxiety takes work, and it is not something you can stop right away. If it was, no one would have anxiety. No one wants to be that miserable!

5. Myth: Anxiety means a teen is weak and lazy.

Truth: Okay, who comes up with this crap? People who struggle with anxiety are actually brave and hard-working. You are waking up each day and choosing to battle your scary thoughts and feelings to carry on with your normal life. That takes courage and so much more energy than waking up happy. Sometimes you get overwhelmed and want to hide, but that is not because you are lazy!

6. Myth: Anxiety is a result of unresolved childhood issues.

Truth: This myth is a half-truth. Some people are anxious because of things that happened in their childhoods, but that is often not the case. As I said above, there is usually something in your DNA that makes you more likely to struggle with anxiety. However, there are plenty of people who had great childhoods who struggle with anxiety too!

7. Myth: Anxious children and teens are shy.

Truth: There is a difference between anxiety and being shy. A shy person makes an active choice to avoid being social, and they are comfortable spending time away from people. An anxious person usually wants to hang out with friends or go to parties, but their anxiety holds them back. I talk to people all day long as part of my job, so people can't believe that I used to be terrified to go to parties. I am not shy. I just got anxious and my anxiety overwhelmed me

8. Myth: Anxiety looks the same in everyone.

Truth: Okay, hopefully you know this is not true. Remember the fight-or-flight response triggered by our amygdala? Some people get angry and aggressive when they are anxious, while other people want to run and hide, and there are all kinds of responses in between. There are many different symptoms of anxiety, and they will show up differently in each person. Your personality has a big effect on what kind of anxiety symptoms you have.

9. Myth: Anxiety is not real. When it happens, it is just a teen being dramatic.

Truth: Um, no. Anxiety is a medical disorder. It is very real and it has nothing to do with a desire to be dramatic. This, like most of the other myths listed here, is just a way to discredit the importance of mental health. People who say this are just being ignorant (and you can tell them I said so).

10. Myth: Anxiety will resolve on its own.

Truth: Oh, I wish this one were true! But learning to handle anxiety takes time and effort. Ignoring it will not make it go away. It usually requires equipping yourself with knowledge (by reading a book like this!), talking with a counselor, and possibly taking medication.

The next time you hear one of these myths, pause and remember that you know the truth. Now you also understand so much more about your body and how your amygdala triggers your fight-or-flight response. Hopefully, this chapter also taught you more about different types of anxiety as well as some of the main causes. Knowledge is power, and you have learned so much in this chapter that you are well on the way to taking charge of your anxiety forever!

Chapter Two

Different Approaches

"Pain is inevitable. Suffering is optional."
— M. Kathleen Casey

Now that you know a little more about what causes anxiety and the different ways it can show up in your life, we are going to dive into the different methods that can help you combat it. When you finish this chapter, you will know more about three approaches you can use to kick your anxiety to the curb: mindfulness, cognitive behavioral therapy (CBT), and dialectical behavioral therapy (DBT).

I am giving you all the tools I possibly can to help you win your battle with anxiety. Some people use all of the tools, while others prefer to focus on one or two. I encourage you to try them all out so you can learn what works best for you.

Mindfulness

One of the hardest things for me to do is to "Be where my feet are." Most of the time, when you are anxious, your mind is not in the present moment. Instead, you are obsessing over something that happened in the past or you are worried about what may happen in the future. Mindfulness trains your brain to be fully present and aware of what's going on around you at any given moment. It also helps you not be overly reactive or overwhelmed, even when there is tough stuff going on. Mindfulness is a powerful way to fight anxiety.

There are seven principles of mindfulness. Some of these may come naturally to you, while others will take work to learn and apply. Like with most lists in this book, I encourage you to read this one with an open heart and mind. Don't just skim through to gather information like you would in school. Instead, take time to really think about each of these attitudes and ask yourself, "How could learning about this make my life easier and happier?"

<u>The Seven Key Attitudes of Mindfulness</u>

1. Beginner's Mind

The first time you do something, your mind is usually open to learning and trying new things. But when you become more comfortable with a new skill, your mind may close itself off. Keeping a beginner's mind means being open and curious about the world around you and not getting stuck in a rut of thinking that you know everything. (I always think I know everything. I am wrong a lot!)

2. Non-judging

Many people with anxiety are really hard on themselves. They get mad at themselves for not being in control of their feelings. This ends up just making things worse. Judging yourself and others can cause a lot of harm. Learning to be nonjudgmental involves calmly acknowledging what is going on without trying to label it or put a value on it.

3. Trust

This is a hard one for many anxious people to grasp. You have to trust yourself and your feelings. That includes realizing that it is okay to make mistakes. Mindfulness will help you learn this important skill.

4. Patience

A lot of anxiety comes from wanting something to happen right away. When you're forced to wait, you get uncomfortable and upset. Patience means allowing life to unfold in its own time without getting worried or anxious about the pace of things. This takes a lot of practice.

5. Letting Go

Your mind may hold on to a thought, emotion, or memory so strongly that it plays it over and over in a loop. Mindfulness teaches you to let go of those repetitive thoughts so that you can have a calm mind and enjoy greater peace and happiness.

6. Acceptance

Life will be hard and challenges will come and go.

Our job is to learn to accept things as they are. Once you accept the reality of a situation, then you can begin to work with and through it. However, if you spend all your emotional energy resisting and denying something, then you'll just exhaust yourself. You will just end up tired, with the same problems.

7. Non-striving

Mindfulness teaches us to pay attention to what is unfolding around and within us without trying to force or change anything. Many anxious people are very goal-oriented and focused on success. Then they get anxious as they worry that they'll never achieve their goals. Learning about non-striving can help you change this pattern so that you can achieve your goals without harming or straining yourself along the way.

Hopefully, you're already starting to see how mindfulness can help you manage your anxiety. Mindfulness shows you how to become still enough to be totally aware of the present moment. In that calm state, your mind is much less likely to jump to anxious thoughts about the past or future. And, if it does, then mindfulness also teaches you to let them go and return again to the here and now.

Mindfulness provides you with a new way of relating to everything in your life, including your anxiety. You learn to notice, accept, and let go of anxious thoughts instead of fighting against them. You have probably learned by now that when you fight with anxiety, you just end up getting more and more exhausted and overwhelmed. Mindfulness provides a better way to handle those anxious moments.

There are three really beneficial mindfulness techniques that I want to share with you: visualization, breathing, and meditation. Each of these is a powerful tool to help you manage and overcome your anxiety. In this chapter, I'll give you an overview of what these techniques are all about. Later in the book, I will share more examples and exercises so that you can practice each of these tools and become comfortable with them.

Visualization

Imagine that you are at the beach listening to the waves hit the shore and feeling the sun kiss your skin. Now close your eyes for a moment and really soak in that experience. What does the beach smell like? Is there a spray of water hitting you as the waves crash to the shore? Can you feel that beach vibe growing within you? Do you notice that you're a little calmer and maybe have a smile on your face? That is the power of visualization. I spend a lot of time on the beach in Hawaii this way, with no fear of sun damage!

There have been many studies that show that visualizing yourself in nature or in another comfortable place can actually make you feel less anxious. All you have to do is pick the place where you feel most at ease. Then picture yourself there, trying to really experience that location with all your senses: What do you see? Taste? Smell? Hear? Touch? Visualization is most powerful when you get all five of your senses involved. The next time you're feeling anxious, spend five minutes imagining yourself in that safe space. You'll be amazed at how quickly it can calm you down.

Breathing

Mindful breathing is a simple practice that can have a really big impact. This method of breathing has been proven to reduce stress and promote happiness. Deep breathing calms down your whole body and can help you shift out of fight-or-flight mode. Basically, deep breaths signal to your amygdala that you really are okay and that it can finally calm down!

There are two helpful ways to practice deep breathing. The first is as a daily practice. All you need to do is sit or lie down, set a timer for five minutes, close your eyes, and take deep breaths in and out. Focus your attention on the changes you feel in your body as you breathe. What is going on in your chest and your abdomen? Can you feel the temperature of the air going in and out of your nose? This small daily practice is a powerful tool in fighting anxiety.

The second way to use breathing to overcome anxiety is by using it at the very moment that you feel anxious. When you feel anxiety rising, you can pause and take three deep breaths. In a matter of seconds, you can start to feel your body relax and your mind slow down and refocus on the present moment.

Meditation

When you meditate, you are slowing down and detaching from your anxious thoughts. This helps you reduce worry and become more balanced and calm. There are different kinds of meditation. Some people really like guided meditation, where you close your eyes and listen to someone telling you what to think about or do. There are lots of helpful apps that can provide you with guided meditations. Breathing is another form of meditation, as we discussed above.

Once you start meditating, you may notice that your mind jumps around a lot. That is so normal that there is a name for it: "monkey mind"! If you get distracted by those jumping thoughts, simply acknowledge them and then come back to being aware of your breathing. There is no need to get upset at yourself. As a matter of fact, you can be proud of yourself for catching your mind wandering! Remember, one of the key attitudes of mindfulness is non-judging.

Cognitive Behavioral Therapy

CBT is a kind of talk therapy where you work on understanding your negative thoughts and then reframing them. You start off learning about CBT with a therapist. However, the end goal is to learn to be your own therapist, so the person you work with will encourage you to take a proactive approach to treatment. I spent many years working with different therapists, and I learned so much!

If you've never seen a therapist or counselor before, you may have some questions or reservations about it. One helpful way to think about it is that a therapist is like a coach. Just like it would be tough to become a star basketball player on your own, it can be difficult to overcome anxiety without the help of someone with the experience and training to guide the way.

Some people are afraid of talking to a therapist. Trusting someone new with access to the darkest recesses of your mind is a lot. It definitely takes courage to be real and vulnerable with someone you've just met. I know this can feel scary, but CBT has been proven to help people overcome a number of disorders, including anxiety, so be as brave as you can. You may be amazed at how far that will take you!

According to psychologist Judy Beck, there are ten principles of CBT:

1. In a therapy session, you will identify your thinking patterns and consider how your life experiences may have affected how you think. Thinking about thinking may sound silly, but it can bring some huge insights and breakthroughs.

2. It is important to work with a trusted therapist. Sometimes it takes a few tries to find someone that you are really comfortable with. Don't give up if the first person isn't a perfect fit. There are lots of therapists out there, and it's worth taking the time to find the right one for you. When you find the right person, it feels like you have a powerful friend who is on your side.

3. This kind of therapy is a collaborative effort and requires you to actively participate. It can be hard to open up and share personal things with someone you just met. But the payoffs are huge! So be brave enough to be real with your therapist. Remember, they have probably heard it all before anyways, and if they didn't want to help you with your problems, they wouldn't have become a therapist!

4. CBT is goal-oriented and problem-focused. Your CBT therapist will ask you what you want to work on and will continue checking in with you about it. That is a great way that this book can be used along with CBT therapy. If there is a topic in this book that you want to focus on, bring it up to your therapist, and they will have more exercises and insights for you.

5. You start by focusing on current problems and specific situations. So, maybe if you feel anxious every time you walk into the cafeteria, you will start by working through that specific anxiety. I really like that part of CBT therapy because it means that you can start to see the results right away.

6. The goal is for you to learn to be your own therapist. This kind of therapy is very empowering. You won't need to work with your therapist forever. Instead, they will be

teaching you everything you need to know to help yourself.

7. CBT is a straightforward approach that strives to work through your issue within six to fourteen sessions. If you are hesitant to start therapy, remembering that it will only be for a limited time can give you the courage to try it out.

8. The therapy session is broken down into three parts. In the introduction, you do a mood check and brief review of the week. The middle is for discussing any problems and setting homework. And the final part is asking for feedback.

9. You will learn to identify, evaluate, and respond to your negative thought patterns. This will save you from getting caught in those exhausting thought spirals.

10. There will be a variety of techniques used to help change your thinking, behavior, and mood, so if one of them doesn't work, there are more to choose from!

Dialectical Behavior Therapy

There is a definite overlap between CBT and DBT. Both can be very helpful for people with anxiety, and they each can take place in a group session, individual meeting, or even over the phone. But what makes DBT unique is its focus on mindfulness and acceptance. It helps you develop core mindfulness skills, interpersonal effectiveness skills, and distress tolerance skills, and it helps you relate to the people in your life and find ways to regulate your emotions.

There are seven principles of DBT:

1. Biosocial Theory: This digs into how the environment you live in affects how you think and feel. For example, if you were punished or criticized for crying or showing strong emotions as a child, then you may have a hard time regulating or expressing your emotions when you get older. I wasn't allowed to cry in the house when I was a kid. Now I absolutely hate crying, which isn't helpful because sometimes we just need a good cry!

2. Acceptance and Validation: Remember when we talked about acceptance being one of the mindfulness mindsets? Well, here it is again! There really is something powerful about understanding yourself and knowing that your thoughts and emotions are perfectly normal. You don't have to be perfect to be good enough.

3. Behavior Change: Sometimes our behaviors make our anxiety worse. If you have some self-destructive behaviors, a DBT counselor can help you understand and modify them. You'll learn healthier ways of handling your

emotions. Some examples of self-destructive behaviors are cutting, avoiding/binging on food, and criticizing yourself. Unfortunately, there is a long list of ways to be self-abusive. I hope this book helps you avoid them!

4. <u>Emotional Regulation:</u> Do you feel like you control your emotions or they control you? DBT will help you to better navigate intense feelings. You do this by identifying the emotion, naming it, and taking a step back to decide how to react. For example, imagine you get so angry that you want to throw something; with DBT's emotional regulation skills, you'll be able to pause, calm down, and make a healthier choice.

5. <u>Distress Tolerance:</u> Sometimes anxiety can make you feel like a small problem is actually a huge issue. This is called "catastrophizing." An example of this is if you see a small rash on your arm and start thinking that you have a deadly disease. Distress tolerance helps you to stop this pattern.

6. <u>Interpersonal Effectiveness:</u> Many people find that their anxiety has a negative effect on their relationships. For example, maybe you hide out in your room instead of going to social events. DBT helps you learn to communicate well and form healthy friendships. This also includes learning to express what you feel and

need, which can be tough when you're anxious!

7. <u>Mindfulness:</u> Here we are, back at mindfulness again! This is a big part of DBT. As you learned above, mindfulness involves learning to live fully in the present moment. This helps you stop your spinning thoughts and get out of negative thought loops.

Whew! This chapter covered a lot of material. You're doing great by investing the time and energy to overcome your anxiety. To make sure that you're not wondering if you picked up all the important details in this section, let's do a quick true or false quiz. This isn't for a grade, but rather to show you how much you've learned and maybe give you a nudge to go back and review anything you have questions about.

Mark the following True or False:

1. There are five principles of mindfulness: _____
2. A beginner's mind means you think you know everything: _____
3. CBT helps you understand your negative thoughts and reframe them: _____
4. Mindfulness is one of the principles of CBT: _____
5. You can learn to manage your anxiety with mindfulness: _____

6. Emotional regulation and distress tolerance
   are part of DBT: _____

7. Once you start CBT, you'll be in it forever:

   _____

8. Mindfulness is all about focusing on the
   future: _____

Now that you've learned about mindfulness, CBT, and DBT, I hope you're starting to see how they can help you make significant improvements in your anxiety symptoms. I encourage you to try out each of them to find out what works best for you.

*Quiz answers: False, False, True, False, True, True, False, False

Chapter Three

Overcoming Overthinking

"When you are stuck in your head, you are behind enemy lines with a terrorist."
— Unknown

Have you ever ridden on a merry-go-round? Most children enjoy sitting on the horses as they go up and down and the whole thing spins around. There is usually upbeat music and laughter, and the whole experience is joyful and fun.

But it's a totally different experience when it feels like your thoughts are on a merry-go-round. They spin and spin, faster and faster, and quickly get out of control. Instead of enjoying the cheerful music, you hear repeated worries, relive painful memories, or replay a frustrating encounter over and over again. There is nothing joyful or fun about this kind of overthinking.

This chapter is going to give you the tools to slow down those spinning thoughts so that your mind can be at peace. We'll start with learning about what's really going on in your mind when you're overthinking. Then we'll put that knowledge into use right away with some helpful exercises and challenges to equip you to handle over-thinking with grace and ease.

What the Heck Is Overthinking?

Overthinking involves having repetitive thoughts that are unproductive and unhelpful. When you're over-thinking about the past, it's called "rumination." When you're overthinking about the present or the future, it's called "worrying." But, either way, overthinking involves endless loops of thoughts that stress you out and don't solve anything.

Now, before we get into all the negatives of overthink-ing, it's important to remember that the ability to think is actually a pretty amazing thing. Your brain allows you to learn new information, solve problems, plan ahead, and create all kinds of amazing things. The problem isn't the thinking itself, it's that your thoughts get stuck in a loop that isn't going anywhere. Overthinking is an exhausting amount of thinking that doesn't actually lead to a solution.

When you're overthinking about the past, you are probably fixated on something you regret or a person or situation that you resent. If you did something embar-rassing and you can't stop thinking about it, that is classic overthinking. Another form of this is frequently wishing that you had made a different choice in the past and playing out in your mind over and over how much better everything would be now if you had made that choice. (I still occasionally do this after I have an argument so that I can win it in my mind. I am still a work in progress too.)

You can also overthink in the present. This may look like focusing on what you don't like about yourself and telling yourself about your perceived character flaws over and over. It can also take the form of always questioning if you're doing the right thing. These thoughts make it hard to enjoy the present moment.

Overthinking about the future can involve short-term concerns like worrying that you'll fail a test. You can also have long-term concerns like wondering if you'll ever find a partner or land a good job. Those worries make you sad and stressed and don't get you any closer to reaching your goals.

There are countless problems that come from over-thinking. Oftentimes, overthinking is focused on decision-making, both wondering if you made the right decisions and worrying that you won't. The crazy part is that all of that overthinking actually makes you more likely to make a poor decision!

One of the most common times to overthink is when you're lying in bed at night. Many people have trouble falling asleep because their thoughts are spinning too much. It can be like you have a committee in your head holding a meeting about your life. I call mine the "Itty Bitty Sh!#ty Committee." Overthinking often causes poor sleep, which I'm sure you noticed leads to low energy, poor focus, and low motivation.

Okay, by now you may even be overthinking about overthinking! So let's stop and look at some common signs of overthinking. This list can help you figure out if you're an overthinker. And, if you are, you're in luck, because later in this chapter, I'll give you a bunch of helpful tools to stop this anxiety-inducing habit.

Ten Signs That You're an Overthinker:

1. You ask yourself a lot of questions that start with, "What if . . ."
2. You relive your mistakes over and over again.
3. You have trouble falling asleep because your brain just won't shut off.
4. You try to find hidden meaning in what people say or what you see.
5. You repeat conversations in your head and think about what you should or shouldn't have said.
6. Sometimes an embarrassing memory may pop in your head and then you can't stop thinking about it, even if what you're remembering happened years ago.
7. If someone upsets you, you have trouble letting it go. You hold arguments with them in your head and say all of the things you would

have said if you had thought of them in the moment.

8. You worry about things you can't control, which, to be clear, is pretty much everything outside of yourself. (We can certainly *try* to control our surroundings, but often we are unable to control people, places, or things.)

9. There are times that you're not aware of what is going on around you because your mind is stuck in the past or the future.

10. When your mind gets spinning, you don't know how to stop it.

If this list made you realize you may be an overthinker, you are not alone. I struggled with overthinking for years! It is exhausting and frustrating. But, thankfully, I learned the tools to overcome this unhealthy pattern, and you can too. I'll share more about those tools at the end of this chapter. But first, I want to tell you more about another kind of thinking pattern that can make you feel more anxious.

Cognitive What?

A cognitive distortion is a negative thought pattern. There are many different types of cognitive distortions. They can all make you more anxious and cause you to have low self-esteem and poor motivation.

You probably already guessed that Cognitive Behavioral Therapy deals with cognitive distortions. CBT helps you take those negative thought patterns and replace them with more helpful ones.

There are twelve main cognitive distortions. Which ones bother you the most?

1. Control Fallacy

Someone struggling with a control fallacy thinks that they are responsible for things that are out of their control. This would be like thinking that you could have somehow prevented a friend from getting into a car accident after they left your house. You are blaming yourself for something that you couldn't have changed no matter how much you wanted to. This can cause major anxiety and frustration.

2. All-or-Nothing Thinking

This is also sometimes called "black-or-white thinking." Basically, it means that you see everything as either good or bad or as a success or a failure. This can cause some real problems when you're a normal human being who makes mistakes. Someone with all-or-nothing thinking will take one mistake as a sign that they're a failure. This will knock their confidence and make them less motivated to keep trying.

3. Labeling

Labeling is an extreme form of all-or-nothing thinking where you apply that thinking pattern to other people. So, if someone says one mean thing to you, then you label them a jerk. Every time you interact with them in the future, you assume that that label you gave them is accurate, so they have no room to redeem themselves.

4. Double Standard

This involves having different standards for yourself versus others. For example, maybe you're quick to understand when someone else makes a mistake, but you refuse to let yourself off the hook if you do something wrong.

5. Overgeneralization

When people overgeneralize, they reach a conclusion about one situation and then incorrectly apply it to many other situations. For example, it would be an overgeneralization if you fail a math test and decide that you'll never understand math, or if you have a bad breakup and you conclude that you just aren't good at relationships.

6. Mental Filters

Mental filters are the opposite of overgeneralizations, but they hurt just as much. A mental filter involves looking at one small event and ignoring everything else. For example, maybe your mom says one critical thing to you along with ten kind things, but all you can think about is that one negative comment. This will make you angry at your mom and pretty bummed out overall.

7. Discounting the Positive

If you discount the positive, then you brush off all your successes as just dumb luck. You refuse to acknowledge the skill and hard work that helped you succeed. When you do well, you assume it was an accident and don't give yourself any credit.

8. Emotional Reasoning

This is the false belief that the way you feel is a reflection of reality. So, if you wake up feeling anxious, then you truly believe that something bad will happen. Of course, it is very important to validate and express your emotions. But it's also valuable to look at rational evidence.

9. Magnification

Magnification is like looking at your mistakes through a magnifying glass while also shrinking down any of your successes, so your negative qualities look huge while your positive ones seem tiny. This habit just gets worse over time because you see everything bad that happens as "proof" that you're a failure and you ignore everything good that occurs.

10. "Should" Statements

Do you want to know one of my least favorite words? "Should!" Yes, I know it seems like a simple, safe word, but I know the truth. "Should" used to rule my life. I could never rest because there was always something else that I "should" be doing. This made me feel guilty and caused me to see myself as a failure because I could never do everything that I "should"!

11. Personalization and Blame

Most situations are pretty complex. But someone with this distortion makes all the outcomes about themselves. So, say you have a group project that gets a low grade. Even though you did your part, you think the low grade was all your fault. You refuse to see that there were other factors involved.

12. Jumping to Conclusions

There are two ways to jump to conclusions: mind-reading and fortune-telling. Mind-reading is when you imagine that you know what someone is thinking. For example, if your friend has a frown on their face, you may automatically assume that they're mad at you. Fortune-telling is thinking the future will happen in a particular way. Often, this assumption gives you an excuse to avoid something unpleasant. It may look like saying, "I am going to fail anyway" as a reason not to study.

Action Items

Okay, enough reading. Let's have some fun!

These exercises and quizzes will help you get to know yourself a little more. You'll be able to apply what you learned to your real life so you can start making some big strides in overcoming your anxiety.

I also included some great journal prompts. Journaling is a really helpful way to get your spinning thoughts out of your brain by putting them down on paper. I suggest getting a fun, colorful journal that makes you smile when you look at it!

Understanding Your Thought Patterns

Did you discover that you have some cognitive distortions? Well, this activity was made to help you identify, understand, and correct your faulty thinking.

Here's how you do it:

1. Pick a specific situation where you experienced a cognitive distortion.

2. Explain how that distortion made you feel. You might use words like "ashamed," "sad," "anxious," "inadequate," or "overwhelmed."

3. Then write out the negative thoughts that came from that distortion. These could be thoughts like "I'm a failure," "This is too hard," or "I can never do anything right."

4. Now imagine removing that cognitive distortion and looking at the situation with a little clarity. What are some different ways that you could think about the situation? Write out those healthier thoughts.

Real or Fake?

Those pesky cognitive distortions can make it hard to tell what's real and what's fake. So, do your best to lay aside false thinking, and look for the truth. Please write the numbers one through ten on a piece of paper and answer True or False to the following questions:

1. I am a bad person.
2. I did something that I regret.
3. I am a failure.
4. I am the ugliest person ever.
5. I didn't perform perfectly at something.
6. I am shorter than some people at school.
7. I am not loveable.
8. Everyone is better than me.
9. Someone got mad at me.

10. I could've done better on that exam.

Hopefully you answered "False" to statements 1, 3, 4, 7, and 8. Those are all cognitive distortions. Next time you're struggling, try to reframe your thoughts to statements more similar to 2, 5, 6, 9, and 10

Four-Step Journal

Okay, now it's time to pull out that pretty journal and enjoy some reflection time. This exercise is a powerful tool to help you understand your negative thoughts and identify which ones cause you the most distress.

<u>Step 1</u>

Write down a negative thought that you had today.

<u>Step 2</u>

Answer these questions:

- When and where did you first have that negative thought?
- How often did you think about it afterward?
- Is this a common pattern for you?

<u>Step 3</u>

Write about how that thought and situation made you feel.

<u>Step 4</u>

Now go back and do the first three steps for other common negative thoughts that you have. When you have at least four to five of them, try to group them by theme. For example, if you notice a theme of thoughts about "always" or "never," put those together. If you notice repeated negative descriptions of yourself, put those together. Just search for any way to link the thoughts. The next time you have one of those thoughts, think, "Oh yeah, here is another one of those 'always or never' thoughts."

You Be the Judge

Sometimes it can be hard to tell if a thought is accurate or not. This exercise will help you put your thoughts on trial and come away with a verdict.

1. Write down the thought.
2. Pretend like you are defending that thought. Put down any evidence that supports that thought.
3. Now act like the prosecutor by listing out evidence against the thought. You should only include facts, so leave off any guesses or opinions.
4. Finally, be the judge and decide if the thought is fair and accurate.

My Rules

Everyone has rules that they live by. There are helpful rules like "It's wrong to lie." But there are also harmful rules like "If you make one mistake, you're a failure." Many people never stop to question or consider the truth behind their own rules. Taking the time to do this may free you from some harmful rules you've been living with.

Start by writing down one of your rules. Then ask yourself the following questions:

- Where did the rule come from?
- What are the advantages of keeping the rule?
- What are the disadvantages of keeping the rule?
- Will you keep, trash, or modify the rule?

Putting Things in Perspective

So many anxiety spirals start with the question, "What if?" This activity can help you stop that harmful line of thinking in its tracks.

- Write out one of your "What if?" scenarios:
- Assess its validity:
- Has this ever happened before?
- How often does this happen in real life?
- Look at the highs and lows:
- What is the worst possible outcome of this scenario?
- What's the best possible outcome?
- Assess your abilities:
- What would you do if the worst possible outcome happened?
- Be your own best friend:
- What would you tell a friend who was struggling with this concern?

A Week of Gratitude

Okay, it's time to bring out that beautiful journal of yours once again. On top of each of the next seven blank pages in your journal, I want you to write one of these gratitude prompts. Then, each day for the next week, take a few minutes to write about what you're grateful for by filling out that day's prompt! Gratitude can go a long way in making you feel less anxious.

<u>Gratitude Prompts</u>

- Day 1: Who is your favorite person in the world? Write what you admire about them.
- Day 2: What is a struggle that you have overcome? How has this made you a stronger person?
- Day 3: Look outside and find three natural objects that you find beautiful. Write down what they are and explain what you love about them.
- Day 4: What are four things you can do this week to make someone else happy?
- Day 5: Name five things that make you smile.
- Day 6: What is the last thing that made you laugh really hard?
- Day 7: What's your favorite smell? How do you feel when you smell it?

The Chair Exercise

This might seem weird at first, but it has helped a ton

of people, so it's definitely worth a try! I don't know about you, but I talk to myself all the time, so this exercise comes really easily to me.

1. Find a quiet place where you won't be bothered by anyone. Put two chairs there and have them face each other.
2. Think about a decision or situation that you are currently overthinking. Make each chair represent one side of the argument. For example, one chair might represent "I should stay in soccer" while the other represents "I should leave the team."
3. Sit on one chair and explain that side of the argument.
4. Switch seats and talk about the other side of the argument.
5. Keep switching chairs, speaking freely, and letting yourself unload all of that internal anxiety.
6. When you have nothing left to say, stand between the two chairs and take a few deep breaths. Thank yourself for being brave, speaking your truth, and taking a powerful step to overcoming overthinking. Even if you haven't found your answer yet, you have made real progress toward finding it!

Breath Awareness

Your breath is a powerful tool for handling anxiety. I'm going to walk you through a simple breathing exercise that you can turn to any time you feel anxious. I do this regularly, and it is remarkable how much it helps!

1. Close your eyes and focus on your nose for three deep breaths.
2. What does the air feel like as it goes in and out?
3. Is it warm or cool as it goes in?
4. Does the temperature change as it goes out?
5. Now focus on your belly for three deep breaths. Simply notice it rising and falling.
6. Take three more breaths. On the in breath, think, "I am strong," and on the out breath, think, "I am calm."
7. Open your eyes and notice how you feel.

Way to go, working through those exercises! A lot of anxiety can be traced back to overthinking. Working through these exercises will help you start to take control of intrusive thoughts and work to overcome your anxiety. Return to them again the next time you catch yourself overthinking.

Chapter Four

Understanding Your Triggers

"Triggers are like little psychic explosions that crash
through avoidance and bring the dissociated, avoided
trauma suddenly, unexpectedly, back into consciousness."
— Carolyn Spring

Imagine if you could stop your anxiety before it started.
Or what if you could notice it when it was just a small
seed of worry and squash it before it grew any bigger? You
can do this if you learn to understand your triggers.

A specific trigger is something in the present that
reminds you of a painful event in your past and causes a
strong emotional reaction. These kinds of triggers can even
make you feel like you are reliving your trauma all over
again. If you suffered from abuse or experienced a trau-

matic event, triggers may even cause flashbacks. The classic example is when a former soldier hears a car backfire and suddenly feels like they are back in a war zone. They feel the same rush of terror they felt when they were fighting the enemy, even though they may only be filling their car up with gas.

However, you can also have more general triggers, which are things that heighten your overall anxiety. They may not be tied to events in your past. Instead, they are emotions, words, activities, or situations that make you more nervous. Everyone experiences different triggers, so what triggers you may not trigger me. This chapter will cover a broad range of possible triggers so that you can discover and name your triggers. This is the first step to finding ways to work with and through them.

How to Understand Your Triggers

Triggers get their name from the role of a trigger on a gun. When you pull the trigger, the gun goes off. It happens quickly and, once the trigger is pulled, there's no going back. This is often how it feels when you encounter an emotional trigger. Suddenly, out of seemingly nowhere, you get upset and worried. People who weren't triggered like you were may look at you in confusion. They don't understand why you suddenly went from "fine" to "absolutely *not* fine." If you've ever felt like this, then you were probably triggered.

When you're triggered, you may do or say things that you will later regret. This is because being triggered messes with your ability to think clearly and act wisely.

Sometimes being triggered is called "emotional hijacking" because it's like someone takes over your ability to control your emotions.

Let's look more generally at triggers that can heighten anxiety.

<u>Fighting</u>

If you were around fights a lot as a child, you may be triggered by any situation that makes you feel tense. When young children are exposed to fighting in the home, they can start to think that they're the cause of it. They feel like they are troublemakers who make every situation worse, or they tell themselves that if they behave perfectly things will get better. Then, any time they're in a tense situation, that feeling of being "tainted" will return to them.

<u>The Media</u>

If you have anxiety, then there's a good chance that you also suffer from low self-esteem. Examples of low self-esteem include thinking poorly about yourself and believing that you are inferior to other people. Low self-esteem can hold you back in life if you are too intimidated to put in the effort to pursue your goals because you believe you won't achieve them.

People with low self-esteem may struggle with comparing themselves to others. The unrealistic standards of beauty in airbrushed photos can be very triggering. People with this trigger may see a picture of a model and immediately feel like they just don't measure up. (I wish they were required to release the photos of those pictures before they were altered. We would all feel a lot better about ourselves.)

Trauma

Experiencing physical, emotional, or sexual abuse can leave people with feelings of deep shame and displaced guilt. This can make them feel very poorly about themselves and even lead to feelings of self-loathing and repulsion. Anything that reminds them of their trauma may trigger those emotions again.

Caffeine

The beverage you turn to when you need a little pick-me-up may actually be dragging you down. Caffeine can make anxiety worse by causing restlessness, a fast heartbeat, irritability, and shakiness. Caffeine can also lead to trouble sleeping, especially if you drink it in the afternoon or drink a lot of it during the day. If you drink more than two caffeinated beverages a day, feel increased anxiety after drinking caffeine, or notice that you're having trouble sleeping, then it may be time to cut down. You'll need to slowly decrease your caffeine intake over a week or more so your body can get used to the change. It is normal to feel more tired and have a little headache during that time as your body adjusts.

Toxic People

If you're always walking away from a certain person feeling confused, angry, or guilty, then they might be toxic. A toxic person is someone who causes distress through their harmful words and actions. They can be really hard to be around, and they can make your anxiety worse.

Toxic people trigger anxiety because they will often put you down and try to make you feel bad about yourself. They also tend to be manipulative and make you feel guilty if you don't go along with what they want to do. Your anxiety may cause you to deal with feelings of self-doubt and low self-esteem, and toxic people can make these emotions ten times worse.

Sometimes it can be hard to identify toxic people, especially if you've been around them for a long time. You may have gotten used to their bad behavior. To help you with this, I put together this list of eleven characteristics of a toxic person to help you discover who is toxic in your life.

1. They won't admit their mistakes.
2. They lie a lot.
3. They blame you for anything that goes wrong.
4. They ignore your boundaries.
5. They act like your feelings aren't valid.
6. They are nice to you but mean to the people around you.
7. They don't listen when you talk.
8. They talk mostly about themselves.
9. You feel crazy when you're around them.
10. You are exhausted after spending time with them.
11. You never know which version of them you're going to get.

If this list helped you to identify a toxic person in your life, it may be wise to limit your time around them. You can also consider trying to talk to them about how their behavior is affecting you. Avoid blaming them and don't resort to name-calling. Please don't call anyone toxic to their face! I don't anticipate that going well. Just be straightforward and say things like, "When you do ___, I feel ___."

If talking to them doesn't help, there are some other ways that you can protect yourself from their toxicity. The first thing to do is set clear boundaries and stick to them. Be straightforward about what you can and cannot do for them. Next, try your best to stay out of their drama. They may try to drag you into it, but stay calm and remember that it's not your job to fix their problems. Finally, focus on overcoming your anxiety instead of trying to address whatever is going on with them. I like to remind myself that toxic people's problems are "not my circus and not my monkeys."

Social Media

Social media can be a great way to stay in touch with friends, and everyone loves watching a ridiculous video or sharing a funny joke together. But there can be a downside to social media too. It can be a trigger for your anxiety.

Have you ever posted something online and then sat there worrying that no one would like it or comment on it, or that the comments would be unkind? You are not alone. A lot of teens struggle with anxiety over what they share online, and their self-esteem can suffer if they don't get the response they want.

Seeing other people's posts can also make you jealous about what they're doing or can make you feel bad about yourself in comparison. Unfortunately, a lot of mean stuff is said online, and you may fear having someone post a mean comment about you. There is a lot of drama on social media, and that can definitely heighten anxiety too.

Start to notice how you feel during and after your time on social media. If you realize it is making you anxious, here are some tips on cutting down:

- Turn off notifications: So many people jump to react when they hear any noise from their phone. That means that the phone is in control. Put yourself back in control by cutting down on the number of messages your phone can send you.
- Stay off screens for an hour before bed: If you're used to scrolling in bed, this will be hard at first. However, after a while, you'll notice that you sleep better and you're spending less time on social media. Many people see a reduction in anxiety when they take this one simple step!
- Enjoy life offline: Make time for your hobbies and your friends in real life. Let these become your focus and your biggest source of entertainment and fun. None of us want to be

in a world where everyone is so focused on their phones that they never learn to dance, play piano, make pasta by hand, build a tree fort, write a book, or any of the other forms of art that people have discovered in an effort to stave off boredom. Boredom inspires creativity.

<u>Family Problems</u>

It can be so hard to live in a tense house. I am so sorry if you're living through that right now. Being around people who are on edge and fighting can naturally make you more anxious. And if you've lived through your parents divorcing, that can be a major source of anxiety. The stress of family problems can lead to you feeling insecure and having trouble trusting people.

If you're seeing a counselor, I highly encourage you to talk with them about your family problems. If you aren't seeing a professional therapist, now is a good time to talk to your school counselor or a friendly teacher. Find someone to talk to, though, because keeping it inside will only make things worse!

<u>Academics</u>

School stresses out a lot of teenagers (and plenty of adult students too!). The pressure to succeed can be intense. Some people even struggle with perfectionism because they feel like a lower grade makes them a failure. It can feel like your entire future is riding on the grade you get on today's math exam. Yikes! That would freak anyone out. When you start to feel yourself getting sucked into school stress, take a moment to pause, and remember that you are more than your grades, your future is more than your grades, and your life is worth more than your grades. It may take a while for you to shift away from a perfectionistic mindset. This would be another great thing to talk about in therapy!

Sometimes people's reaction to academic stress is to give up on school entirely. They decide to skip classes, avoid homework, and even drop out of school completely, thinking that those things will reduce their stress. Just the opposite! These things make them even more likely to run into trouble in the future. The stress of avoiding your responsibilities can make life just as hard as being a perfectionist does. This approach all but guarantees even more stress in the future, but it can be easy to forget that when you're in the middle of your current situation.

My Triggers

Now that you understand a little more about triggers, it's time to do some exercises to figure out how much these triggers are affecting your daily life and equip you with the resources to deal with them.

Analyzing Situations

Think back on the last time you were really anxious. Got it? Okay, now I want you to think about what happened right before you felt anxious. Try to describe the event in detail. Where were you? What was said? Who else was there?

Now write down the consequences of getting so

anxious following that event. These consequences could be both positive and negative. My anxiety about having friends over, for example, causes me to get my house extra clean before anyone arrives. Also try to think about whether the consequences occurred right away or were delayed.

You are starting the hard and important work of connecting your triggers to your responses. Try to do this every time you feel anxious. Soon enough, you'll have a good list of your triggers. This information will help you start to prepare for and handle your triggers in more constructive ways.

Trigger Mapping

In this exercise, we're comparing your trigger responses to an elevator. When you're triggered, the elevator shoots right up to the top floor. This is your initial reaction to the trigger. Then the elevator moves down a floor, and you experience a more vulnerable feeling. Each floor that you go down accesses deeper emotions until you finally come to the basement. This is the core wound that you can trace back to your childhood. It is the whole reason you were triggered.

For example, you could be triggered by someone pointing out a mistake. Your initial reaction on the top floor is to deny it. The floor below is when you feel anxious and wonder if they're right. Below that, you think, "If he's right, then I am not good at this." The next layer is to think, "If I am not good at this, then I am not worthy." The floor under it is when you think, "If I am not worthy, then I am not lovable." Finally, you hit the core wound in the basement: "If I am unlovable, then I'll be alone and unloved forever."

Okay, now that you're in the basement, it's time to think back through your life and try to find your earliest memory of when you felt this way. Maybe you remember missing an important catch in a Little League baseball game and feeling like your father was disappointed in you. This taught you that love was conditional and dependent on your performance. That was the original wound where this whole trigger began.

Now it's your turn to map your trigger. First, write your trigger. Then add the top-floor reaction. Next comes the fourth-floor reaction, then third, second, and first-floor reactions. Finally, write out the basement core wound and the original wound.

Once you get down to an original wound, it can take time and therapy to let that wound begin to heal. It probably won't happen nearly as quickly as you want it to, but try to remember that these feelings didn't develop overnight, so it will take a minute for them to get better. In the meantime, you can catch yourself in those top-floor reactions and remind yourself of what is really going on beneath the surface. This puts you in control of your emotional reaction.

State-Shifting

This is the practice of shifting out of a triggered state. The main point is to not react right away when you are triggered and instead to give yourself time to calm down enough to react more wisely.

There are four steps to the state-shifting practice:

1. Name it: Tell yourself that you are triggered. You'll need to know your body's clues well enough to catch yourself when you're triggered. Your body is going into fight-or-flight mode. Some common signs include an upset stomach, a clenched jaw, defensiveness, emotional outbursts, judgmental thoughts, or a foggy mind.

2. Make some space: Remove yourself from the triggering situation. A direct way to do this is to let the other person know that you're feeling emotional and need some time to collect your thoughts. An indirect way to do this is to go to the bathroom or say you need to check on something. Just let yourself move away from the tense environment so you can clear your head.

3. Actually shift your state: Now you need to get out of fight-or-flight mode and help yourself calm down. There are many different ways to do this, including deep breathing, meditation, exercise, or listening to music. Remind yourself that you are safe and that you don't need to fight or run away.

4. <u>Deal with the situation:</u> Okay, now that you've calmed down, you need to decide whether any action is needed. Assess the situation, decide what your goal is, and then act on it. This may include going back into the triggering situation, but now you will be prepared to handle any strong emotions that come up for you.

The next time you feel triggered, go through those four steps: name it, make some space, shift your state, and then deal with the situation.

Triggers are oftentimes unavoidable. But recognizing what your triggers are and how to manage them will help immensely with your anxiety. It may take some time to find and deal with all of your triggers, especially if they've been around for a long time. Remember that you are looking for progress, not perfection. Keep applying these rules and using these tools and you'll be well on the way to feeling less triggered.

Chapter Five

Time-Management Tools

"The bad news is time flies. The good news is you're the pilot."
— Michael Altshuler

Sometimes being anxious can feel like running on a treadmill: you're exhausted and feel like you're going nowhere. And if you have poor time-management skills, it can seem like you're on that treadmill and someone is yelling at you to go faster and faster. No one wants to feel like that!

Learning to manage your time will go a long way toward calming your anxiety. The tools in this chapter can help you get off the treadmill and move forward at your own pace without the pressure of deadlines and the fear of unfinished projects making you feel so anxious. I wish they taught us time management in school because it is a skill that will help you achieve more and feel calmer throughout your life.

Time Management and Anxiety

Anxious people often think they'd feel better if they just had more time to do everything. But the truth is that everyone gets the same twenty-four hours in each day. It is up to us to learn how to organize and plan our time to get everything done. Thankfully, time management is a skill that we can learn. Just like any other skill, it will take some practice to get used to it. But soon enough, you'll be handling your time like a pro!

Time-management skills include prioritizing, scheduling, goal-setting, focusing, and organizing. Another big part of time management is learning to stop procrastinating. Please don't feel bad if that's something that you have a hard time with. It's a pretty common issue, and I'll give you the help you need to handle it in a better way. The exercises at the end of this chapter will provide powerful tools to help you grow your time-management skills.

When you learn to manage your time well, you will feel like you have more time to deal with whatever is worrying you. And the research shows that you'll also sleep better, have less stress, and be less anxious overall. Seriously, learning about time management can help you make big improvements in your life!

There are ten main benefits of effective time management:

1. <u>Less stress:</u> Do you wake up wondering how you'll get everything done and then go to sleep worried that you didn't do enough? Time-management skills will help you face each day with a manageable to-do list and rest better at night knowing how much you accomplished.

It can be really stressful when something goes wrong and a task ends up taking more time than we anticipated. Good time management will show you how to schedule extra time in your day and remain calm if plans change. This means that overall you'll feel calmer and minor delays and setbacks won't have the power to stress you out.

1. <u>More free time:</u> Your schedule should always include time for rest and relaxation. Once you know how long your tasks will take and can plan ahead for when you'll complete them, then you will start to see some time opening up in your schedule. Then you have the freedom of choosing to spend your time on things that make you happy, like hobbies or hanging out with friends.
2. <u>Increased productivity:</u> Wouldn't it feel great to get more done in less time? This can really boost your confidence and self-esteem. You'll feel good knowing how much you're accomplishing.

3. <u>Better focus:</u> An anxious brain is often a scattered brain. You feel pulled from thought to thought and task to task. Learning to focus on one thing at a time will help you slow down and actually finish what you started.

4. <u>Clear goals:</u> Anxiety can make us feel like our goals are too far away for us to ever reach them. But good time-management skills will show you how to set small daily goals that leave you feeling accomplished and excited about being one step closer to your bigger dreams. There are some common mistakes that many people make when setting goals. Later in this chapter, we'll go through the steps necessary to set the best possible goals. Then, in the exercises at the end, I'll walk you through how to set goals for your life.

5. <u>Easier decision-making:</u> Do you change your outfit multiple times before you walk out the door? Yup, that used to be me too. Imagine how much time and energy you would save if you could make decisions more quickly. Many anxious people have trouble making decisions. The tools in this chapter can help you be confident enough to make decisions and not second-guess yourself.

6. <u>Great reputation:</u> People tend to think highly of those who can commit to something and

follow through with it. The people around you will trust you as someone who will do what you say you will.

7. <u>More confidence:</u> It feels so darn good to check a task off your to-do list. Just that simple little check mark can make you feel more confident about your ability to handle the next task that comes your way. I will provide you with some to-do list templates at the end of this chapter.

8. <u>Better work:</u> Rushing to finish at the last minute doesn't lead to the best work. But once you learn these time-management skills, you'll be able to take the time to review your work before you turn it in. This will improve the quality of your work overall.

9. <u>Achieve goals faster:</u> Waiting is hard. We all want to reach our goals right away. Time management helps you move more smoothly and quickly toward your goals. When you have the joy and satisfaction of achieving a goal, then you will be so happy that you learned these skills.

Goal-setting is a big part of time management. This includes learning to align your daily activities with your bigger life goals and arranging your priorities along the way.

Effective goals are SMART. This acronym stands for **S**pecific, **M**easurable, **A**ttainable, **R**elevant, and **T**imely.

- **S**pecific: Good goals are written clearly so that there's no confusion about what you're trying to do.
- Bad example of a specific goal: I need to get in shape.
- Good example of a specific goal: I will be able to run a 5k.
- **M**easurable: The most powerful goals answer the questions of how many, how much, and/or how often you will do something.
- Bad example of a measurable goal: I'll study hard.
- Good example of a measurable goal: I'll study algebra for one hour a night for the next three nights.
- **A**ttainable: Your goal needs to be something you can actually achieve. Don't set yourself up for disappointment by making the goal too big.
- Bad example of an attainable goal: I'll be an NBA star.
- Good example of an attainable goal: I'll become a starter on the varsity team.
- **R**elevant: It's wise to set goals that are in line with what you're really trying to do. They need to be part of the bigger picture.

- Bad example of a relevant goal: I'll catch thirty frogs so I have the experience to become a vet.
- Good example of a relevant goal: I'll volunteer at a local animal shelter so I have the experience to put on my vet school applications.
- **T**imely: When will you achieve your goal? Put a date on the calendar and stick to it. The best goals have a clear endpoint.
- Bad example of a timely goal: I'll finish the project soon.
- Good example of a timely goal: I'll finish the project by Friday at 3:00 p.m.

Let's look at one more example of SMART goals:

- Non-SMART goal: I will feel more confident at prom.
- Make it **S**pecific: I will lose weight.
- Make it **M**easurable: I will lose ten pounds.
- Make it **A**ttainable: I will lose ten pounds by not having soda or fast food.
- Make it **R**elevant: I will lose ten pounds by not having soda or fast food so I feel more confident at prom.
- Make it **T**imely: I will lose ten pounds by May 1 by not having soda or fast food so I feel more confident at prom.

- <u>SMART goal:</u> I will lose ten pounds by May 1 by not having soda or fast food so I feel more confident at prom.

Can you see how much clearer the SMART goal is compared to the non-SMART goal? By taking the time to clarify exactly what you are aiming for, you've already given yourself a clear picture of what it will take to get there.

Understanding Your Time Management

How do you spend your time? Many people only have a fuzzy idea of how to answer that question. And if you don't know how you spend your time, that means you're not in control of your schedule. It's a lot harder to reach your SMART goals without being able to manage your time. This activity will show you how you spend your time so that you can start making smarter decisions about it.

Begin by drawing a big circle that fills up a whole piece of paper. Next, draw lines dividing the circle in half from top to bottom and then from left to right. Now divide each of those four sections in half again and again until, in the end, you'll have a big circle broken into twenty-four slots. Each slot represents one hour.

The next step is to fill in the circle with everything that you do on a normal weekday. If you sleep on average six hours a night, fill in six slots with the word "Sleep." Then fill in a circle slice for how many hours you spend at each of your other activities like school, sports, clubs, eating, driving, video games, hobbies, time with family and friends, etc.

Take a while to look at that circle and think about how you spend your time.

Is there anything that you wish was written on the circle?

Is there anything on the circle that is just a waste of time?

Write out your top ten priorities from most (1) to least (10) important:

Are those priorities reflected in how you spend your time?

Okay, now draw the same circle with the same twenty-four slots again. This time, fill it in with your ideal schedule that reflects your true priorities. In a perfect world, would you get eight hours of sleep? Put that on this ideal circle. Do you love to paint but never have time for it? Put that in this circle.

Take some time to compare the two circles. Notice the differences and start to dream about how you could make your dream circle into your actual circle. Get curious about what is possible and start to imagine how great you will feel when how you use your time is in line with what you prioritize.

How will you change your daily schedule as a result of this exercise?

Time-Management Log

Okay, based on what you learned from the circle exercise, you're going to write out your new daily schedule.

Get excited! This is where you take what you learned and turn it into action items. In addition to writing out what you do every hour, you'll also classify every activity on a scale of 1 to 4.

1: Urgent!

2: Important

3: Somewhat important

4: Not important

Break down the time, activity, and importance level of each of your daily activities. For example:

- Time: 7:00–8:00
- Activity: Get up, eat breakfast, get ready for school
- Importance: 1

Now write out your whole daily schedule.

Do this for a whole week. Then look back on the week and see how many "not important" (level 4) activities filled up your time. Make a commitment to decrease those and increase the more important ones. For many people, this means less time watching TV or playing online. While those things aren't bad and it is important to rest, if you're doing too many unimportant activities, you're likely missing out on some of the much more important level 1 and 2 activities that would benefit you much more. Remember, it's all about balance!

Morning Meditation

Meditating in the morning can help with your time

management. It allows you to start off the day feeling less stressed and thinking more clearly. Meditation calms the mind down so you can make smarter choices and regulate your thinking patterns.

I know setting the alarm a little earlier can seem daunting. But the good news is that your morning meditation can be as quick as five minutes. Once you get used to a shorter meditation and all of its great benefits, you may want to lengthen your practice. For now, start slow and give yourself something simple to cross off your to-do list as soon as you wake up. This will help you build momentum and start the day off on a positive note.

Your first decision is where and when to do your meditation. You want to be in a quiet area that is free from distractions. I encourage you to add some fun touches to make your environment feel cozy, like gentle music, soft lighting, essential oils, or a comfy pillow. Make it special—this is your time. Then decide when you'll do this every morning. Will it be at 7:30, right before breakfast? Remember to make the goal specific!

Now, when you sit down to meditate:

1. **Sit:** Find a comfortable place to sit up straight. This may be on the floor, on a couch, or in a chair. Take a moment to notice what it feels like in the spots where your body touches the floor. Relax into that sensation.

2. **Set a timer:** This could be a normal phone timer, or you could use an app like Insight

Timer. These apps give you a gong or bell sound to close out your practice.

3. **Relax your body:** Take a few long and slow deep breaths to release tension and let go of any worries. During these breaths, let your attention start at your head and slowly move down to your toes. Relax any tight areas that you notice along the way.

4. **Focus on your breath:** Now pay attention to your breath and how it moves through your body. Observe the air in your nose, the rise and fall of your chest, and the movements of your belly. Just notice what it feels like to be alive this morning.

5. **Return to center:** You will get distracted by thoughts or sensations. That is normal. When you catch yourself being distracted, just return back to your breath. Rather than beating yourself up for drifting off, be proud of yourself for catching it! I try to say to myself, "Good job—you noticed that!" and then focus again. Continue noticing your breath until the timer goes off. Remember that there is a reason they call it a "meditation practice." If anyone were a master at it, they would call it a "meditation perfect!"

And that's it! Five easy steps in five minutes. Commit to doing this simple meditation daily and enjoying all the wonderful benefits it brings. It takes about a month to really get used to a new habit, so I encourage you to commit to doing this five-minute practice every day for the next month. You can make a calendar with checkboxes for each day. After you do your morning meditation, check it off and feel good about this investment you're making in yourself!

Setting Goals

Earlier in this chapter, we reviewed how to set SMART goals. Now is your chance to put this training into practice.

What is one of your top goals?

Why is this goal important to you?

Is this goal . . .

- Specific?
- Measurable?
- Attainable?
- Realistic?
- Timely?

What might hold you back from completing this goal?

When will you achieve this goal?

What are the small steps that will take you from where you are right now to where you want to be when you reach this goal? List out your action items and when you'll achieve those smaller goals.

. . .

You've made great strides in preparing to reach this goal! Put your plan into effect and then celebrate when you reach the goal. Then it's time to do the activity over again for your next goal. Soon, it will become second nature to think through all the steps that will help you achieve your dreams.

To-Do Lists

A to-do list is a simple time-management tool. It will help you stay organized and on track to meet your goals. These lists can also help you remember when things are due and stay on top of your commitments. Using one of these lists every day will help you avoid getting distracted by competing interests. It will also protect you from getting disappointed or discouraged because you'll be able to point to all the great steps you've already taken toward your goal instead of being overwhelmed by the rest of the steps that remain.

If you want to make your own to-do list, grab a piece of paper and write "Today's Goals" at the top. Then leave enough space to write three goals. Divide the rest of the paper in half from top to bottom. On the left side, write "Schedule," and on the right side, write "To Do." You'll use the schedule side to write out what you'll do that day, noting both the time and the activity. So, it may say, "8:00 a.m. to wake up" and so on with what you'll do that day, all the way up until "10:00 p.m. to go to bed." The right side is where you will list out all the tasks you want to accomplish that day.

Keep practicing making SMART goals, setting daily

to-do lists, tracking your time, and doing your morning meditation. Over time, you'll see how proper time management can reduce a lot of your anxieties. And remember that no one expects you to do each of these items perfectly. It's all about growth and the courage to try new things. You're learning and growing so much, and I hope you're proud of yourself for facing your anxiety head-on.

"Realize that you are not alone, that we are in this together, and most importantly that there is hope." — Deepika Padukone

One of the very first things I acknowledged in the introduction to this book was that although anxiety affects a huge proportion of young people, many feel like they're the only one who feels this way. Think about how you viewed yourself before you picked up this book... Did you feel like you were alone? Did you look around at your friends and classmates and feel like everyone else had it under control? So many teenagers feel this way, and it can be incredibly isolating.

If you wish that you'd realized sooner just how common anxiety is, you have the opportunity right now to let someone who feels just like you did know that they're not alone and that there are things they can do to manage their anxiety. Don't worry, You don't need to talk to a soul... You don't even need to leave your room. All it will take is just a few moments of your time and a few short sentences.

By leaving a review of this book on Amazon, you'll show other teens that they're not alone and that there's information out there that can help them... This in itself is a huge help in their ability to feel better. You can show them how to find the help they need! Thank you for your help. When you know how difficult it is to live with anxiety, it's natural to want to help others in the same situation. https://tinyurl.com/tamingbeast

Chapter Six

Organizational Tools

"For every minute spent organizing, an hour is earned."
— Unknown

There are a lot of people who enjoy cleaning and organizing. I am not one of those people. Though I really do feel better when I am in a tidy space with a place for everything; I used to go to great lengths to avoid being the person who actually did the work. Now that I have lived in the world for a while, I realize how much time I actually save by keeping things together in the first place. I am not saying it is fun now because it is definitely not but I am both calmer and saner in my tidy spaces. As an added bonus, I don't worry about friends stopping by and seeing my mess anymore because there isn't one.

Organization is like a superpower. If you know where everything is, then you don't have to waste time searching for it. Feeling in control of your environment will go a long way toward decreasing anxiety and increasing confidence.

I am guessing that you have, somewhere in your house, a junk drawer where pens, paperclips, random pieces of paper, and other odds and ends are all jumbled together? It isn't easy to find things in a drawer like that, and even looking in it can feel overwhelming. Now compare that to opening a silverware drawer where there are separate compartments for knives, forks, and spoons. You can easily reach in and grab what you need. It's easy and shouldn't make you feel anxious. That is the power of organization!

This chapter will teach you about the benefits of organization. Then the real treasure comes at the end of the chapter, where I'll share some really useful plans and checklists that can help you become more organized.

The Relationship between Organization and Anxiety

Our brains like order—that's just how we're wired. So, if your room, locker, or other parts of your life are disorganized, your brain will begin to protest. It will get distracted looking at all the mess and start to feel overloaded. Remember the fight-or-flight response you learned about earlier in this book? Well, a messy environment can keep your body and mind trapped in fight-or-flight mode. That is why clutter has been proven to make people feel stressed and anxious. Feeling embarrassed and being harassed by family members to tidy things up, isn't exactly helping your anxiety either.

A disorganized room can also lead to problems with sleep and appetite. You will have a harder time falling asleep in a cluttered room than in an organized one because in a cluttered room, your mind is distracted by all the mess. Also, living in a messy environment increases your chances of making poor food choices. There seems to be a connection between taking care of your environment and taking care of yourself. Clearly, there are some serious consequences to being disorganized.

Mess leads to stress! Here are eight reasons why:

1. A messy environment overwhelms your senses.
2. A messy environment makes it harder to relax.
3. A messy environment can make you feel guilty and embarrassed.
4. A messy environment takes your attention away from what you should be focusing on.
5. A messy environment makes you frustrated because you can't find things quickly.
6. A messy environment tells your brain that there's always more to do.
7. A messy environment inhibits your creativity.
8. A messy environment makes you anxious.

So, yeah, you've got to take care of the mess if you want to get a handle on your stress. Some people get trapped into thinking that they're not organized people and then they let that hold them back from fixing the messy places in their lives. Organization isn't a character trait, it's a skill! That means that you can learn it. And luckily, it is pretty easy to learn the basic organizational techniques needed to fight clutter and create a more peaceful environment. I'm going to teach you the best ones over the next few pages.

But first, let's look at a few other ways that being disorganized might be negatively affecting you. Once you get organized, you may start to see improvements in these areas too. Be on the lookout for the positive effects that come from getting organized. This will keep you motivated to stay organized.

Organization issues can lead to poor grades. You could be the smartest person at your school, but if you can't keep your assignments in order and keep track of your school supplies, then your grades will suffer. Lack of organization will also make it harder to plan and prepare for your next test or project. Imagine how good it would feel if your grades went up just because you were better organized!

Your family can also be negatively affected by poor organization. Is your mom always bugging you to clean your room? Does your dad get frustrated when you put off a big project until the last minute? Do you feel anxious about showing your grades to your parents because you know they'll ask why you didn't perform better? What if organization could improve all of that?

Many teenagers feel like their parents are always

nagging them. And two popular nagging topics are messy rooms and poor school performance. Learning to be more organized can help with both of those issues.

Okay, hopefully by now you're convinced that organization is important. So, let's jump in and learn this important skill. We're going to focus on three main areas: your bedroom, locker, and binders. Commit to yourself right now that you will set aside an hour or so to get these places in order. It will be time that is well invested.

Bedroom Organization Plan

Your bedroom should be your safe space, and just walking into it should make you feel calm and relaxed. If that's not the case, then you have some organizing to do! You spend a lot of your life in your room, so making changes to this space can have far-reaching effects on the rest of your life.

We're going to walk through your room, focusing on one area at a time:

<u>Nightstand</u>

Take everything out of your nightstand. Once it's empty, wipe down the drawers. Now take a look at the items from your nightstand. Decide which ones really belong back in there. First, think about what needs to go on the top of the nightstand. This usually includes a lamp and possibly an alarm clock or something you're reading. You want the top of your nightstand to be clutter-free, so only choose what's absolutely necessary.

Next, look at how many drawers you have in the nightstand and assign each one a purpose. For example, you might have one drawer of essentials that includes things like lotion, a journal, a pen, a flashlight, and lip balm. If you have a second drawer, you can use it for storage or for items that you use less frequently.

Bed

What is lurking under your bed? Take the time to pull everything out. Put away anything that doesn't belong. Decide what you will store there. This can be a good place for out-of-season clothes, shoes, extra sheets, and seasonal items or things you don't use very often. They sell special boxes that are made to fit under the bed. You can also get a bed skirt to hide anything you store down there.

Dresser

Okay, take a deep breath before diving in. You can do this! Let's start by emptying out each drawer. Now wipe down the whole dresser. Next, look at each item and ask yourself when the last time was that you wore it, how you felt when you wore it, and if you think you'll wear it again. If you haven't worn it in over a year, feel uncomfortable in it, or don't think you'll wear it in the future, then get rid of it! You can donate items that are in good shape to charity.

Once you've gone through the whole dresser, decide what will go in each drawer. Many people put undergarments and socks in the top drawers, then have a drawer for shirts and another for pants. Decide what makes the most sense for you.

Just like you did with the nightstand, only put items on top of the dresser that need to be there. This might be a jewelry stand, a framed photo, or something else that makes you smile when you look at it.

<u>Closet</u>

You're doing great! I know this is a lot of work, but it will pay off big time when you're enjoying the rewards of a more organized life. Once again, the first step is to take everything out of the closet. Then go through and ask yourself the same questions that you did with the clothes in the dresser: Have you worn it in the last year? Do you feel comfortable in it? Do you plan to wear it again? If you answered no to one or more of those, then it could be time to get rid of the item. Get a bag for donations (for items that are in decent shape) and another bag for trash.

With everything out of the closet, now is a good opportunity to clean it out by wiping down shelves and vacuuming the floor.

Now divide your items into these groups:

- Shoes
- Scarves and belts
- Bags and purses
- Sweaters
- Dresses
- Shirts
- Pants

Put them back in your closet in their groups so you'll always know where each type of clothing is located when you need it next.

Room Check

You're almost done! The last step is to walk around your room and look for any hidden areas of clutter or mess. Clean those spots and find a home for the random odds and ends that you come across.

Congratulations! Your room is now organized. That took a lot of work and you should be proud of yourself for putting in the effort. Take a few moments to sit in your lovely room and notice what it feels like to be in a clean, organized room. Remember back to what it was like when your room was messy. Do you notice any difference in how the state of your room affects you?

Now you just need to remember to put things away in their new places so that everything can stay neat and tidy. It's normal that when you get busy, your room may get messy again, so it can be helpful to designate one day of the week as your reorganization day. This is the day every week when you'll do a mini version of this exercise by quickly evaluating your nightstand, under-bed space, dresser, and closet and putting away anything that is out of place.

Locker Organization Plan

Now that your room at home is organized, it's time to get your spot at school set up too. Start by making a list of all the items that belong in your locker. Here are some ideas to get you started:

- Backpack
- Lunch box

- Textbooks
- Notebooks
- Pens and pencils
- Loose papers
- Folders
- Clothes
- Small stuff
- Other items particular to your hobbies and school activities

Now decide where you will keep each of those items. Write out your plan and commit to leaving your items in their designated spots.

Here are some ideas:

- <u>Backpack:</u> Hung on a hook.
- <u>Lunch box:</u> Placed on a shelf.
- <u>Textbooks and notebooks:</u> Lined up and standing up straight on the bottom of the locker.
- <u>Pens and pencils:</u> In a small bag.
- <u>Loose papers:</u> Sort through them and have a folder for each class to file them in or throw away what is no longer needed.
- <u>Folders:</u> Make sure these are clearly labeled and you know what belongs in each of them. Organize them into one larger folder or binder that contains them all. Then put this folder or binder somewhere in your locker. If there's

room, it works well to have it standing up next
to your textbooks and notebooks.

- <u>Clothes:</u> Hung on hooks or folded on the top
  shelf.
- <u>Small stuff:</u> Organize any extra items such as
  lotion, lip gloss, or other things on the top shelf
  or get a small bag to put them in. Your goal is
  to avoid having small things get lost in the
  shuffle.

The final touch to your organized locker is to decide
what to tape up on the inside of it. On the practical side,
it's wise to have a copy of your schedule placed there, and
a monthly calendar can be helpful. On the fun side, you
might want to hang up a photo that makes you smile or an
inspirational quote that keeps you in a positive mindset.

Binder Organization Checklist

One of the messiest parts of many teenagers' lockers is
their binders and notebooks. This can cause serious problems when you're trying to study or do homework because
you'll spend too much time getting frustrated that you
can't find what you're looking for. So, now that you've
made the huge effort to organize your room and locker,
let's take the final step and get those binders in shape.

Follow these binder rules:

- One binder for each subject. Put the course
  name and class information on the front cover.

- The class syllabus should go at the front of the binder so you can refer to it quickly when needed.
- Organize binders using dividers with labels on them.
- Include some loose paper or a notebook in each binder for taking notes.
- Don't stuff loose handouts in the binder. Instead, everything should be hole-punched and put in the rings.
- Make sure all of your papers are dated and kept in chronological order.
- Write your name and contact information somewhere on the binder.

These notebook rules will help you stay organized:

- Have one notebook for each class and put the course name and information on the front cover.
- If there are dividers in your notebook, make sure they're clearly labeled.
- Don't let loose papers clutter up your notebook. Instead, take the time to put them where they go.
- Keep your notes dated and in chronological order.
- Make sure you can read your notes! Okay, this is a hard one for me because I have terrible

handwriting. But I've learned that taking a few extra seconds to write something clearly will really pay off in the long run. So, when you're taking notes, I encourage you to write clearly.

- Put your name and contact information somewhere on the notebook so someone can return it to you if it gets lost.

You have just put in a lot of time and effort to organize these major parts of your life. And if you haven't finished organizing your room, locker, or binders, I encourage you to do that before you move on to the next chapter. Remember that organization is not a "one-and-done" kind of thing. You'll need to stay committed to putting things back in their place and will probably need to make time to clean out your room once a week. But, once you see how much better you feel when you're organized, you'll feel more motivated to keep it that way.

As I mentioned earlier, stress and anxiety have been linked to living in messy, disorganized environments. So now you get to enjoy the feelings of calm and ease that can come from living in a more organized space.

Chapter Seven

Dealing with Food Anxieties

"Food can become such a point of anxiety—not because it's food, but just because you have anxiety. That's how eating disorders develop."
— Vanessa Carlton

Eating is necessary for our very survival. That's why it is so important to recognize your current relationship with food and make sure you're relating to food in a positive way. If you do have a negative relationship with food, then it is really important to address that. This chapter will help you do so.

You probably know that food can nourish or damage your *physical* health, but food (and your relationship to food) can also nourish or damage your *mental* health. Does food make you anxious? Do you feel like you are in control of your relationship with food? Do you feel like it is in control of you?

I went through my own struggle with disordered eating in high school. At the time, a lot of things in my life felt out of control, and food was one thing I could be in charge of. Before I knew it, I was obsessed with controlling my food. Part of me thinks I would have been taller if I hadn't been so hard on my body at such a critical time for growth. It took me years to get my food issues under control. Hopefully, this book will help you find some tools to avoid that scenario and create a healthy relationship with food now.

If you have some anxiety about eating, this chapter is for you. Just like you can have a fight with your best friend and then make up with her, I'll talk you through ways to improve your relationship with food. And if you already have a positive relationship with food, that is wonderful! You can still learn a few things here.

The Relationship between Anxiety and Eating

Food is part of our everyday life, no matter how we feel about it. Think of the people you see every day, like your parents and neighbors. Some of those people may make you feel good, so you go out of your way to see them often. And you may dread seeing others, so you do whatever you can to avoid them. But if you see people every day, you eventually form *some* kind of relationship with them, for better or worse.

The same is true of food. It's always there, so we can't help but develop a relationship with it. The relationship we develop can be like a relationship with a good friend, where food is a source of satisfaction and positivity. Or food can cause anxiety, where we dread each meal, resent having to eat at all, and wish the whole idea of eating would just go away and leave us alone.

How does this happen? How does something like food, something that is meant to be good for us, become something that leaves such a bad taste in our mouths (see what I did there?) There are many factors that lead to food anxiety. Some of the most common include social media pressure, negative self-talk, genetics, personality traits, and community and cultural messages. As we explore each one, think about how these have affected you:

- <u>Social Media Pressure:</u> Having your life and everyone else's on constant display can be a nightmare, especially when most of what appears on social media has been edited or photoshopped. It is easy to feel shame and get shamed. People also like to post about their food and their bodies. These can be triggers if you have an unhealthy relationship with food.
- <u>Negative Self-Talk:</u> The most influential words we hear are those we tell ourselves. If you believe that your body is not how it's "supposed" to be and tell yourself that, it can lead to a really unhealthy relationship with

your body and the food that fuels it. Changing self-talk is challenging but totally possible. A lot of the mindfulness exercises in this book will help you to be more aware of those negative thought patterns.

- <u>Genetics:</u> Remember how anxiety can be genetic? The same is true for your body shape and size. Your genetics dictate a lot of who you are.

- <u>Personality Traits:</u> Some people are naturally more laid-back while others constantly feel the pressure to succeed. If you're a perfectionist, then you might always be judging your body and trying to change it.

- <u>Community Messages:</u> Some groups emphasize bodies and food differently. For example, in athletics, there may be many natural discussions about nutrition and body shape, which can easily lead to self-consciousness.

- <u>Cultural Messages:</u> Our society promotes beauty standards that are hard to live up to. We see super-skinny models who have undergone surgery to look the way they do. Then we look at our own natural bodies and feel like there's something wrong with us. This is damaging and painful.

- Sexual Abuse: Unfortunately, many of us have had to deal with some form of sexual misconduct imposed upon us. There is often a direct correlation between sexual abuse and food anxiety. Sometimes we try to hide ourselves by either becoming really thin or making ourselves less of a target for sexual attention by gaining a lot of weight. Neither of these approaches works, but both make us feel like we are "doing something" about the situation.

If you have a good relationship with food, you may enjoy cooking and eating, or you may just not think about food much at all. If you have a poor relationship with food, you may feel awkward about eating in front of other people or may be self-conscious about how much you eat. There is nothing wrong with feeling anxious about food. The problem comes when that anxiety starts to control what you eat. You can develop a toxic relationship with food. This is called an eating disorder.

There are multiple kinds of eating disorders:

- Anorexia Nervosa: People with anorexia may believe they are fat even if, in reality, they are dangerously thin. They may stop eating entirely, skip meals, only eat select "safe" foods, obsessively weigh themselves, or exercise way too much. If untreated, anorexia can lead to brittle bones, growth of thin hair all over the body, dry hair and skin, exhaustion, and even organ failure.

- <u>Bulimia Nervosa:</u> Bulimia involves eating an uncontrollable amount of food (binging) and then vomiting, taking laxatives, fasting, or exercising excessively to get rid of the food. This can lead to many health problems and a very damaging relationship with food.

- <u>Binge Eating Disorder:</u> Those with binge eating disorder will eat way too much food, but they don't purge afterward like those with bulimia. People with this disorder are frequently overweight and feel shame about their eating and their body size.

- <u>Orthorexia:</u> People with this disorder become so obsessed with healthy eating that it actually becomes unhealthy. They have a very limited number of foods that they think are safe to eat and become upset when those foods aren't available. Eventually, they will cut out multiple food groups, which robs their bodies of the nutrients that they need. This disorder leads to many unexpected health issues including intestinal trouble, hair loss, skin issues, and many other problems.

It's important to know that people struggle with eating disorders for a number of reasons, one of which may be food anxiety that has gotten out of control. However, just because you feel anxious about food does not mean you have an eating disorder, and food anxiety does not guarantee that you will develop an eating disorder.

If you are reading this chapter and believe you may have an eating disorder, please talk to someone you trust and seek medical and professional help. This chapter is meant to help with food anxiety, but it is not a cure for any medical or psychological condition, including eating disorders.

You Are What You Eat

Anxiety and food often go hand in hand. We've talked a lot about being anxious about food. But did you know that certain kinds of food can also increase or decrease your overall anxiety level?

Certain foods can trigger anxiety symptoms. If you have food anxiety, it may be better for you to minimize or eliminate your consumption of these foods:

- Sugary foods
- Fried foods
- Processed foods
- Food additives/food dyes
- Caffeine

Yes, I know that that list may include some of your favorite foods! Don't try to cut them all out at once; the healthiest and best diet changes happen slowly over time. Choose one category and slowly decrease it. Once you decrease one of these food triggers, work on reducing the next one. Keep checking in with yourself to see how you feel. You'll likely start to realize that foods that tasted good on your tongue may have been making your anxiety worse.

Knowing what *not* to eat is only half of the equation, of course. If you have food anxiety, what *should* you eat? What foods are going to work for you and help you? There are many that you can try to add to your menu. Here are a few that I recommend:

- Salmon
- Chamomile
- Turmeric
- Dark chocolate
- Yogurt
- Eggs
- Pumpkin seeds
- Brazil nuts

Again, awareness is key. Check in with yourself to see how foods make you feel. Then choose those foods that make you feel good. This is a great way to take control of your health and happiness!

Ultimately, everyone has to deal with food. And if food is a source of anxiety for you, that means you have to deal with it too. By examining your relationship with food and making informed choices about what to eat and not eat, you can turn a source of anxiety into a source of nourishment and empowerment.

Let's look at some basic resources to get the ball rolling.

Eating Disorder Self-Assessment

Eating disorders are serious business. To determine whether you need to seek professional help, answer yes or no to the following questions based on how you feel *today*. Write down your answers if you need to since we'll count up your total number of yeses at the end.

1. I use diet pills to control my weight.
2. I have tried so many diets that I can't remember them all.
3. I am extra aware of my intake of fat, carbohydrates, and/or calories.
4. I have recently lost and/or gained more than thirty pounds.
5. My mood depends on feeling in control of my weight or eating.
6. I feel guilty if I eat too much or eat foods that I think I shouldn't eat.
7. There are certain "unsafe" foods I try to *never* eat.
8. I hide foods or lie to others about how much I actually eat.
9. I feel unable to stop eating once I take my first bite.
10. There are parts of the size and shape of my body that I hate.

11. I use food to comfort myself or escape from my problems.
12. I regularly skip meals or go a day without eating at all.
13. My habits of eating and exercising isolate me from other people.
14. It's hard for me to talk about how I feel or know how to deal with my emotions.
15. I spend a great deal of time thinking about food and planning what and when to eat.
16. I avoid social situations if they involve eating.
17. I worry about getting fat.
18. If I don't exercise, I don't feel right about the day.
19. I sometimes vomit after meals or use laxatives to control my weight.
20. 20. If I could just get to my goal weight, I know I would feel better about my life.

Well, how many did you answer yes to? The higher the number, the more likely it is that you should consult a doctor and/or mental health professional. Only they can determine if you have an eating disorder and advise about the best next steps.

My Inner Dialogue

Most of us have thoughts passing through our heads throughout the day to help us solve problems, remember things, or take mental notes of our situation. Have you ever stopped to evaluate what that inner dialogue sounds like for you? Sometimes this voice speaks in a harsh or judgmental way and sounds like an inner critic. Sometimes it speaks in a loving, patient, compassionate way and sounds like an inner advocate.

Both of those inner voices serve a purpose. Our inner critic helps us learn from mistakes and avoid bad decisions. Our inner advocate reassures us that life isn't over if we fail and encourages us to keep going. If we make space for both, we can enjoy an inner balance and healthy reflection. But if one gets a lot louder than the other, we may get thrown off. Are you used to hearing from your inner critic more than your inner advocate? There is a very mean voice in my head sometimes that can take over if I don't watch it. It is the very worst when I am Hungry, Angry, Lonely, or Tired. When I find myself being aggravated, I have to check in to see if I am one of those four things. I have to make a point of listening to my inner cheerleader instead.

Does your inner critic sound like it's shouting or blocking the voice of your inner advocate? If so, you may need to practice making space in your mind for the inner advocate. If you grow in this skill, you can learn from what your inner critic is trying to show you without dealing with the harshness and blame games it would otherwise try to play.

Sometimes it's hard to decide who is an inner critic and who is an inner advocate, especially if you've never heard of these concepts. This exercise will help you understand this better.

Consider the following critical statements. For each of them, try to think of a gracious, compassionate response. If it's hard, use the lead-in words provided to start.

Compassionate Alternatives

When you catch yourself with critical thoughts, try to think of an alternative explanation.

- Inner Critic (IC): "If you go to the buffet, everyone will watch how much food you get and what choices you make. They'll judge you for it."
- Inner Advocate (IA): "Are you sure? Another possibility is . . ."

Nonjudgmental Observations

We often judge ourselves pretty harshly. Try to take a step back and just make an observation about what is happening without attaching a judgment to it.

- IC: "Everyone else got a salad, but I ordered a burger and fries! They're healthier than me. How embarrassing. I am acting like such a pig!"
- IA: "When I looked around, I noticed that . . ."

Practicing Curiosity

Instead of being scared about new things, try being curious.

- IC: "My friend's parents made us dinner, but I've never had this before. It may or may not be healthy. I wish I knew if this food was safe or not!"
- IA: "How interesting! I wonder . . ."

If your inner critic has been being mean to you, now is the time to help your inner advocate find its voice. Whenever you notice your inner critic being rude or judgmental, try to think of something kind and compassionate to say in response. It may feel weird to talk to yourself like this, but once you get the hang of it, you'll realize the power of giving your inner advocate a stronger voice.

I'm Good Enough

Those were some sample situations that may or may not sound familiar. But whether or not we deal with those specific situations, we all have an inner advocate and an inner critic. So what things do you hear from those voices in your own life? Think of ten inner criticisms that are true to your own experience and write them down.

When you hear from the critic, does your inner advocate respond? If so, write down what you tell yourself. If it's hard to hear from the advocate, try using some of the skills and prompts above (compassionate alternatives, nonjudgmental observations, practicing curiosity) to formulate responses.

What Matters to Me

Consider the following list of values. All of these have their place in life, but some will matter more to us than others. Pulling from the following list, begin by picking ten values that seem important to *your* life.

Once you have selected your ten values, rank them by putting the numbers 1–10 to the left of each of the values you chose. Your highest value should be ranked #1, and the next most important #2 . . . all the way through to #10.

There are no right or wrong answers here. This isn't about what your parents value or what you think you should value. Now is the time to be 100% honest about what is important to you.

Values:

Animals/Pets

Creativity (Art/Music/Writing)

Organization/Structure/Routine

Spirituality and Religion

Academics, Education, and Grades

Social Media Following/Influence

Romantic Relationships

My Ethnic/ Cultural Identity

Physical Health

Personal Relationships (Friends/Family)

Productivity and Meeting Goals

Beauty/Fashion/Image

Safety and Protection

Taking Care of Myself

Being in Nature

Financial Gain and Security

Taking Care of Others (Volunteering/Serving)

Mental and Emotional Health

Relaxation/Rest

Hobbies and For-Fun Activities

Nutrition/Cooking

Now that you've identified your values, take some time to really think through them. Answer the following questions:

- Why are these values important to you?
- When did they become important?
- Who influenced you to value these things?
- Were any of your selections or rankings driven by anxiety or your inner critic? How so?

Breaking the Cycle

When anxiety gets out of control, it can become a vicious cycle. "Cycle" comes from a word related to "circle" and describes the feeling of going around and around through patterns of behavior. We may recognize one of these patterns but be unable to stop it.

When you are stuck in a cycle of anxiety, your anxiety controls your actions. You may feel out of control and unable to get a handle on your emotions. If you've ever felt like that, I am so sorry. I know how hard that feeling is. That's why I included this exercise to help you break that anxiety cycle.

Imagine that you have a friend named Dana. She is self-conscious about eating in front of other people, so she avoids social situations where she has to eat, like lunch at school. Instead of eating with everyone else, she sneaks food from her locker in between periods and sometimes eats in the locker room. This leads to feelings of isolation for Dana and questions from her peers.

Think about the flow of feelings, behaviors, and effects.

The problem of food anxiety leads to the anxious thought about people watching her eat.

This thought leads to the anxiety-controlled behavior of eating in secret.

And that behavior causes Dana's peers to question her, which reinforces her anxiety about eating in front of people.

This cycle goes round and round, often becoming worse over time.

Dana's peers enjoy her company, want to spend more time with her, and miss her at lunch. They want to be polite and include her, so they eventually ask her why she never eats with them. When Dana hears this question, it reinforces her fears and suspicions that she is being watched and judged, making another trip through the cycle more likely.

And the cycle goes on and on . . . *unless* we have the tools and empowerment to break it. It may not happen all at once, but we can take small steps to chip away at the hold anxiety has on us.

For example, Dana could choose one or two friends she feels most comfortable with and begin eating lunch with them. Perhaps she starts eating lunch with friends two days a week. As she grows in confidence, she can build up the courage and comfort to dictate her own eating habits rather than letting her food anxiety dictate them.

My Cycle

Do you feel caught in a cycle? Think about your problem, the anxious thought that goes with it, the anxiety-controlled behavior it causes, and how it is reinforced.

Breaking My Cycle

Now brainstorm possible cycle-breaking behaviors that could help you chip away at any control your anxiety has over you.

Write out three ways that you can loosen the hold anxiety has on your eating habits:

Body Scan

Anxiety about food may be related to the anxiety we have about our bodies. As we loosen from anxiety about our food/bodies, that does *not* mean we stop thinking about them; it means we make sure that we are hearing from *both* our inner critic and inner advocate about our food and bodies.

One way to give room for your inner advocate to tell you about your body is a mindfulness technique called a "body scan." This is when you set aside intentional time to be still, be quiet, and give compassionate attention to how your body feels and what it may need from you. There are many body scan meditations online that you may enjoy, but here is a basic outline to try for yourself. It can be done in as few as ten minutes.

- Create a peaceful, comfortable environment.
- Dim the lights.
- Turn off noise-making distractions (TV, speakers, phone alerts).
- If possible, request to not be disturbed during your scan.
- Close your eyes to filter out visual distractions.
- Lie or sit on a comfortable surface.
- Place your hands in whatever manner feels most natural.
- Take a few moments to just breathe. "Breath" will be a unit of time throughout this exercise.
- Take an intentional deep breath. Then notice all the places where your body is making contact with a surface.
- Do these points of contact change as you inhale or exhale?
- Imagine gravity pulling you down and the surface pushing you back up. You are being held.
- Start with your head, and move down section by section to your toes.
- Spend at least three "breaths" in each place, but take as many as you need.
- What sensations do you feel? These may include tension, buzzing, numbness, tingling,

aching, burning, pressure, relaxation, twitching, pins and needles, or anything else.

- There are no right answers! Practice nonjudgmental observation. Your goal is to notice rather than evaluate.
- Your attention may wander. If so, notice this and gently return to your scan.
- Mindfulness takes practice. Be gentle with yourself. You will not be focused the entire time. It's normal to get distracted. Just keep gently returning your attention to your breath and body.
- When you reach the end of your body scan, "zoom out" to remember your whole body again. Gravity is pulling you down. The surface(s) are holding you up. You are being held.
- Use your last deep breath to open your eyes and return to the present moment.
- Consider the sensations you noted. Is your body telling you something?
- Move into the rest of the day with this mindfulness.

4-7-8 Breathing

In our most anxious moments, we may feel like our thoughts are attacking us. Being stuck in an anxious thought cycle is like being stuck on a roller coaster or trapped in a speeding car. It is like your thoughts hit the gas pedal of your mind and make your mind race. As we already learned, Anxiety does the same thing to your heart as it beats faster and your lungs as you breathe more quickly and shallowly to try to catch up.

In those frantic and overwhelming moments, you need to get back to the basics, and nothing is more basic than breathing! By channeling your energy and focus into controlled, disciplined breathing, you can hit the brakes for your body *and* mind, so neither one gets out of control. When you anchor yourself into a controlled, intentional breathing pattern, your heart rate calms down, your breathing slows and deepens, and your mind will gradually slow down to a speed where you feel comfortable in the driver's seat once again.

The beautiful thing about breathing exercises is that we can use them anywhere and any time! A quick go-to exercise is 4-7-8 breathing. To employ this technique, use the following steps:

- Inhale through your nose at a slow, steady pace for **four** seconds. (I like to count one, one-thousand, two, one-thousand, three ,one-thousand, four, one-thousand.)
- When you are done inhaling, hold your breath in your lungs for **seven** seconds.
- Then exhale slowly and evenly through your mouth for **eight** seconds.

Easy, right? Repeat this three more times for a total of

four cycles and then reassess how you feel. You can do this entire exercise as many times as you need.

Mindful Eating

Confronting food anxiety is a way to regain control over your thoughts, your food, and your thoughts *about* food so that your thoughts don't gain control of you. We can't go on forever living in fear of our own thoughts or in fear of food.

Many of the exercises in this chapter deal with our mental approach to food and eating. But at some point, we have to get into the practical reality. We are human. We eat. So what about the process of buying, preparing, and eating food? What does healthy control look like then?

The answer lies in the idea of *mindfulness*, a state of being where we are focused on the present moment and able to calmly acknowledge our feelings, thoughts, and bodily sensations. Use the following practical steps to help yourself select, prepare, and eat foods in a mindful way.

1. <u>Connect the Dots.</u>

Consider the health value of the foods you buy or order and how they make you feel better or worse for eating them. Do you recognize when some foods make you feel sluggish? Unpleasant? Tired? Imagine where you would find these foods in a grocery store, and stick to what you would find in the produce and fresh food sections . . . not what would come out of a box or bag.

1. <u>Hunger Good. Hanger Bad.</u>

Let your body tell you when it's time to eat, and listen to it! When you follow your body's cues, you can make healthier decisions and exercise self-control. When you wait too long to eat, you become so eager to fill your stomach that you pay less attention and lower your standards about what goes in.

1. <u>Shrink Your Plate.</u>

Literally. Eating on a smaller plate takes the guesswork out of portion control. Use a smaller plate but fill it up as much as it will hold, then challenge yourself to make it last until the very end of mealtime. This will ensure that you have sensible portions and don't overwhelm your metabolism by eating too fast.

1. <u>Practice Gratitude.</u>

Your family may say grace or have some kind of routine before the first bite is taken. This can be very helpful for mindfulness. Pause and reflect on what it took for your food to make it to your plate. Did someone grow it? Who prepared it? How far was its journey to get to you? Who is there to share it with you? Give thanks for every part of your meal.

1. <u>Be a SENSE-ible Eater.</u>

Mentally record how your food impacts all five of your senses. What is the texture? How does it smell? Can you hear it rattling on the plate or simmering in the pot? How many colors do you have in front of you? As you taste it, can you try to guess all the seasonings used to flavor it?

1. Eat One (Small) Bite at a Time.

Half the fun (or more) of eating is getting to taste your food. But we can only taste what's on our tongue. If your mouth is too full, you are depriving yourself of an opportunity for mindfulness. If you realize you've been eating on autopilot, put down your fork between bites to break the cycle and restart mindfully.

1. "Chews" Your Own Adventure.

Chew until you can taste every aspect of the food you're eating. Count how many times you chew a bite before swallowing. Is it above or below ten? It may be that the more you chew, the more you taste and enjoy what's in front of you.

1. Slow Down.

You may have realized that the only way to do some of these steps is to slow your rate of eating. That's on purpose! The more time you spend with food, the more you can develop a healthy relationship with it!

Because food is an unavoidable part of life, it has the power to be a great asset or a great obstacle on our path to confronting and controlling our anxiety. If you feel that your anxiety around food has surpassed the point where you are able to exercise control, tell a parent or trusted adult and seek medical attention as soon as you can.

Chapter Eight

Managing Test Anxiety

"I have not failed. I've just found 10,000 ways that won't work."
— Thomas Alva Edison

In the last chapter, we discussed how food anxiety can be tricky since it's impossible to avoid food. There's another unavoidable part of teenage life that is a common source of anxiety: tests in school.

You likely have multiple tests in each class every semester. That makes for plenty of chances to get anxious. If you have test anxiety, you might be tempted to skip school or "feel sick" on test days. But avoiding tests isn't the answer. In fact, it only makes things worse, as you are only delaying the inevitable or settling for a zero when you could have done much better.

So you can't avoid tests, but, thankfully, there are ways to make them less stressful and more manageable. In this chapter, we'll look at what causes test anxiety and I'll supply you with plenty of methods to calm your test anxiety and make test-taking easier.

What Is Test Anxiety?

Imagine this scenario: There's been a test looming on your calendar for a few weeks. You've taken good notes in class, studied hard at home, and even reviewed everything again right before class. But as soon as the paper hits your desk, your mind freezes. You zone out, and your whole body tightens up. You feel a lump in your throat as your shaky hand pulls the paper close. You swallow and start writing, feeling like you're already doomed before you've even started.

Does that describe you? If so, you may have experienced an episode of test anxiety. This is a kind of performance anxiety that sets in when you feel pressure to do well or are worried about negative consequences if you *don't* perform well. Like singing a solo, auditioning for a play, or stepping onto the pitcher's mound, taking a test is a kind of performance.

People without anxiety may think of tests as a chance to prove what they know. So, if they studied hard, they'll walk into a test confidently and zip right through the questions. But, if you have test anxiety, you may fear that taking a test will inevitably expose everything you *don't* know! No matter how hard you prepared, you may think that you're doomed to fail. Then your mind starts spinning with thoughts like "What will happen when I fail this test? I'll die of embarrassment—unless my parents kill me first! And I won't get into college! My life is ruined." Then down the anxiety spiral you go.

Test anxiety affects the body and mind. I've already mentioned the mental "zone out" or "freeze up" effects when your mind doesn't cooperate. But tests can also bring on physical symptoms like stomachaches, headaches, weakness, shaky hands, and sweating. Your heart may beat faster than normal, and you may even hear your heartbeat thumping in your head. An especially strong feeling of test anxiety can make you feel like you are about to faint or vomit. Thanks for being super useful, amygdala . . . *not!*

Dealing with test anxiety is not easy. But once you understand what is going on in your body, you'll realize that you can stop this negative reaction and learn how to walk in to tests with greater confidence.

What Causes Test Anxiety?

Before we talk about the mental and physical sources of test anxiety, let's be very clear about the emotional side of things: it's entirely natural, normal, and common to feel nervous about tests. Knowing we will be graded makes us feel vulnerable. Any time we perform, we want to do well. And, of course, no one wants to fail.

So there's no shame in feeling nervous about a test. However, when that normal, nervous feeling grows to the point that it's affecting your body and mind and making you feel miserable, then it's time to take action. Once you learn the tools to fight test anxiety, you'll feel much better.

Test anxiety, like all other forms of anxiety, is really just about anticipating stress. As we approach stressful situations, like tests, our bodies try to prepare us. On a physical level, our bodies release the hormone adrenaline. This makes us physically prepared for danger and is part of the fight-or-flight response we studied earlier. Adrenaline causes our physical responses to test anxiety: high heart rate, sweating, and stomach tightness. Depending on our stress level, these symptoms can be mild or severe.

Our minds try to prepare us for stress by thinking up possible scenarios so that we can be prepared to handle them. However, this is not always helpful! We find ourselves thinking, "What if I forget everything?" or, "What if I am the only one who fails?" And this makes it really hard to think about the material we studied.

Test anxiety is a physical and mental overreaction to stress. If we don't have a game plan for test day or know how to break the cycle, we can find ourselves in an anxiety spiral at the worst possible time.

Fortunately, that's exactly what this next section is for: preparation and empowerment!

Progressive Muscle Relaxation

If you have test anxiety, you can feel trapped in your seat. Even if you wanted to take a moment to yourself, you may not be allowed to get up and leave. However, you don't have to escape in order to relax. Just like you focused on our breathing in previous chapters, you can use mindfulness to relax your muscles.

Here is a simple practice you can do right in your chair before or during a test to engage your entire body and release tension.

1. As you sit in your chair, conform your body to the shape of the chair. Don't lean forward. Let the chair hold you up. Uncross your arms and legs and put your feet flat on the ground.
2. Take a few 4-7-8 breaths (which you learned in chapter 7), and then do the following to release tension from your head to your toes.

- **Forehead:** Squeeze the muscles in your forehead (like you are glaring or looking *really* confused) and hold this for ten seconds. Feel the muscles tighten. Slowly release this hold over the course of fifteen seconds and feel the tension release. Breathe slowly and steadily and feel this relaxed posture.
- **Jaw:** Bite down to tighten your jaw, then hold for ten seconds. Slowly release the tension and come to a relaxed posture over fifteen seconds. Notice this relaxed posture as you breathe slow and steady.
- **Neck/Shoulders:** Raise your shoulders, like you are trying to touch them to your ears, and squeeze as hard as you can for ten

seconds. Breathe slow and steady as you release over fifteen seconds. Imagine you can feel the tension falling off.

- **Arms/Hands:** Ball both of your hands into fists and clench them tightly enough to make your knuckles white for ten seconds. Breathe slow and steady as you release your hands into a relaxed and open posture. As your hands open, imagine you are literally letting go of any stress.
- **Buttocks:** Pull your buttocks together tightly like you are trying to hold (something) in for ten seconds. Slowly release the tension and feel yourself sink into your seat as you breathe slow and steady.
- **Legs:** Increase the tension in your calves and quads by imagining you are trying to push your shoes through the floor, and hold for ten seconds. As you release this hold, breathe deeply and imagine your legs dangling from the chair holding you up.
- **Feet:** Do the same thing with your feet that you did with your hands. Curl your feet into "fists" and hold this tension for ten seconds. Breathe slow and steady as you release the tension and let your feet be comforted and "held" by the shoes you are wearing.

You may not have time to do all of the above before or

during a test, but think of this list as a "menu" of sorts. You can do an entire body scan, or you can target areas in which you feel the tension more obviously. When your body is at rest, it is easier for your mind to be at rest. And you'll be able to perform better on your test with a relaxed mind.

Red Balloon Visualization

As I mentioned earlier, test anxiety is rooted in the anticipation of stress. Your mind and body are imagining what might go wrong and trying to prepare you for it in ways that may not be helpful to you. With a test on the line, you want your imagination to work *for* you, not *against* you.

So here is a technique to engage your body, mind, and imagination to release unhelpful stress and anxiety. Like the body tension scan above, this can be done right at your desk.

1. As you sit in your chair, conform your body to the shape of the chair. Don't lean forward. Let the chair hold you up. Uncross your arms and legs and put your feet flat on the ground.
2. Bring an imaginary red balloon up to your lips. This balloon has the word "STRESS" written on it in all caps and big, bold letters. Don't worry—nobody can see this balloon but you!
3. Inhale slowly and steadily. Feel each breath coming through your nostrils and inflating your lungs.

4. Exhale slow and steady, and, as the breath leaves your mouth, imagine it is inflating the balloon in front of you with all of the doubt, anxiety, fear, and stress that you were feeling. As you finish exhaling, imagine the balloon floating off into the sky, far out of sight.

5. Repeat this as many times as you need to until you feel calm, centered, and positive.

Test anxiety is a natural extension of being called upon to perform in a way that has measurable and meaningful consequences. There is nothing to be ashamed of if you have test anxiety. This chapter has hopefully helped you to equip your body, mind, and imagination to recenter and put yourself in the best possible position to succeed. (Of course, you'll still need to remember to study!)

As a bonus tip, I want to share a simple technique I have been using for years to address my test anxiety. I quickly read through all of the questions on the test, marking them with a "1" if I know the answer immediately, a "2" if I will know it if I work on it for a minute or two, and a "3" if it is going to be more challenging. Then I go back and answer all of the ones first. After that, I work through all of the twos. Then I can do the rest of the questions (threes) to the best of my ability. With this technique I am not losing time being stuck on problems that I don't know the answer to. This technique significantly increases my chances of doing well on tests!

Chapter Nine

The Beast Known as "Peer Pressure"

"I'm not in this world to live up to your expectations and you're not in this world to live up to mine."
— *Bruce Lee*

When we're born, we don't have much choice over who is in our lives. No one gets to choose their birth family (though, full disclosure -my hippie parents truly believe that we all made agreements with each other before we were born. I do not subscribe to this philosophy!) Then, when we're small children, most of those decisions are made for us. We're enrolled in school, put in playgroups, and maybe taken to church or signed up for different teams and clubs. Eventually, though, we gain more control over our social circles and can actually choose our friends.

Our friends are such an important part of our lives. They're usually the people we want to celebrate with when good things happen and are the people we turn to when we need help or advice. Good friends can even help calm us down when we feel anxious. But sometimes, we can have friends that actually make our anxiety worse. That's what we're going to talk about in this chapter.

Who Are My Peers?

People around our age that we choose to interact with are called our "peers." When you spend time with your peers, you grow closer to them and learn to relate to each other at a deeper level. As you grow up and get more independent, you may spend more time with your peers than with your family. In fact, you may come to think of your peer group as its own extended family.

When you start thinking about the kind of person you want to be in the world (or the kind of person you think you *should* be), your peer group will be pretty influential. The dozens of interactions, conversations, and decisions you each make will impact and influence your lives. You may compare yourself to some peers, compete with others, and look up to a few. Your peers may influence your decisions because you want what they have, because you admire them, or because you fear being left out and not belonging anymore.

In other words, even though you influence who your friends are, it is also true that your friends influence who *you* are.

What Is Peer Pressure?

Your peers influence you in a number of ways. They provide feedback and advice, socialize with you, encourage you, and try new experiences with you. When you experience things together, it helps relationships to deepen and helps bonds to form. As these bonds form, the opportunity for influence grows.

It's important to know that the influence your peers have on you can be positive or negative. On the positive side, peers can pressure you to better yourself, stop bad habits, or take up new healthy activities. When you hear "peer pressure," though, it usually refers to the negative impact that your peers can have on your identity, choices, and life.

When peer influence becomes a source of anxiety and stress, you are dealing with peer pressure. Your peers may try to pressure you into drinking or doing drugs, having sex before you are ready, shoplifting, skipping classes, or making other irresponsible decisions. Peer pressure may be *explicit* in nature, like saying, "Oh, come on . . . everyone else is doing it!" A lot of times, though, peer pressure is *implicit*, which means that it is less easy to see. Your peers may ignore you if you disagree with them, stop inviting you to things after you stand up to them, or turn away from you, making you feel like you don't belong anymore. Even though your head knows that it is probably not worth it to have friends who act like that, it is hard to convince yourself to stay away when they are the group you are used to hanging out with.

Peer Pressure and Anxiety

We naturally find comfort in relationships. Belonging to a group makes us feel safe. Nobody wants to be left out. When we stand out from the crowd or disagree with a group, it's natural to wonder, "What if I am the problem?"

Social media has made peer pressure even harder. People now have much more access to your life and can cause big problems for you through something as simple as an emoji reaction to a post. Many teens feel pressure on social media to make their lives look a certain way, and it can be anxiety-inducing to wonder what everyone is thinking about that picture you just posted.

We may find ourselves constantly comparing ourselves to peers through their posts and "likes." Photo filters can reinforce unrealistic body expectations, making us feel self-conscious. We check our followers and "like" counts and constantly assess whether or not we are being included or excluded. That's stressful!

Even when everything is peaceful, we may not feel settled, anticipating the next potential conflict or fearing the next rejection.

Analyze Risks

Think about everyone you are connected to and imagine those connections like a web. Every day, you move through this complex web as you decide how to interact with the people around you. There can be positive or negative social consequences for each decision you make in that web.

For example, something that makes your friends laugh may disappoint your parents or disrespect a teacher. Or perhaps your friends feel judged that you didn't join them for something, but this choice makes your parents proud. For any given social decision, there is a balance between social risks and social rewards. It can feel like a juggling act!

This activity will help you understand your decisions and their consequences. Thinking through the risks and rewards of a situation is an important way to take owner-ship of your life. Improving your decision-making process can save you a lot of time, effort, and maybe even apolo-gies. Once you learn this skill, you'll find that it's easier to make decisions and that you're happier with the results.

Peer Pressure Situation Exercise

Think about something that you feel pressured to do. Then ask yourself these questions about the social risks and rewards:

Social Risk

1. If you choose to *do* what you are being pressured about, what are two bad things that could happen?
2. If you choose *not* to do what you are being pressured about, what are two bad things that could happen?

Social Reward

1. If you choose to *do* what you are being pressured about, what are two good things that could happen?
2. If you choose *not* to do what you are being pressured about, what are two good things that could happen?

Think through times that you felt pressured in the past and what you did about it. Then ask yourself the following questions:

- Do you respond in a similar way most of the time?
- Do you feel a lot of pressure to do things that could harm you?
- Do your friends encourage you to better yourself?
- What does your decision-making pattern say about your values? (Reflect back to the "What Matters to Me" exercise from chapter 7.)
- What does the pressure you feel from friends/peers say about *their* values?

Trust Yourself

Start by noticing how you feel right now. Is your jaw clenched or your stomach tight? Relax your body from your head all the way down to your toes.

These questions might bring up some strong emotions. That's okay. You don't need to be scared of your emotions.

Just answer the questions honestly with a focus on what this will teach you about yourself.

This first set of questions can be used as a daily check-in to see how well you trust yourself.

<u>Daily Trust Questions</u>

How much did you trust yourself today?

- When did you not trust yourself today? Why not?
- How did your ability to trust yourself affect your confidence?
- How did it affect your relationship with others?

<u>Weekly Trust Questions</u>

At the end of the week, take some time to answer these questions.

What do people in your life trust you to do? How did that happen?

- Are there areas of your life where people treat you like you're not trustworthy? Did something cause that to happen?
- How will you work to trust yourself and help others trust you more in the upcoming week?

Take a Walk to Clear Your Head

If you feel overwhelmed by peer pressure, taking a mindful walk can help you think more clearly. On your walk, try to pay close attention to what each step feels like. In order to do this, you'll need to walk slowly and really notice what it feels like when your foot hits the ground. Then pay attention to how your muscles are working together to move you forward. Spending this time out in nature while appreciating how your body works can help your mind calm down.

My Mantras

Think back to the "What Matters to Me" exercise from chapter 7. As you read the list of values, some jumped out to you more than others. This showed you what you value and what makes you unique. Imagine those values as beads on a string that you wear around your wrist. These are the values you carry with you through life. They affect who you are right now and will guide the type of person you will become.

Sometimes, we need to remind ourselves of the type of person we are. We need to recenter on what we care about. That's where a *mantra* comes in. Think of a mantra as a mission statement. It is a statement that says what matters to you and how you live that truth daily. Your mantra turns your attention back to your values, like touching the beads on your wrist.

Take your five highest-ranked values from chapter 7 and think of a mantra for each of them. Find a way to state how the value helps you. Remember that living this value is an act of self-love and self-trust.

Here are a few examples to help you get started:

- <u>Academics, Education & Grades:</u> I am a learner who is growing in knowledge.
- <u>Taking Care of Others</u> (<u>Volunteering/Serving):</u> When I help others, I make the world a better place. I have a heart full of compassion.
- <u>Physical Health:</u> My body is beautiful, and I care for it well.

Knowing your values and remembering them daily will help you stay true to yourself in social situations. Before you can relate to anyone else or be on anyone else's side, you have to relate to yourself and take your own side.

Peer pressure can cause a lot of anxiety, but if you employ the exercises above, you can relieve this feeling.

Chapter Ten

Four-Step Calm-Down Plan

"Nothing diminishes anxiety faster than action."
— Walter Anderson

Some doctors say that "prevention is the best cure." This means that it's easier to stop problems before they start. For example, the "cure" for dehydration is making sure you drink enough water and don't get dehydrated in the first place.

This is a great principle. But when it comes to mental health, it can be easier said than done.

This book has equipped you to understand anxiety and has empowered you to take control and prevent as much anxiety as possible. As you've worked through this book, you have learned so many effective ways to prevent anxiety. But there may still be moments when your anxiety rears its ugly head. That's normal. No one can avoid anxiety forever. The goal is not to never feel anxious again since that's pretty impossible (and also dangerous since some level of anxiety is helpful in certain situations). The goal is to prevent anxiety as much as possible and to have tools to manage it whenever it returns.

What do you do when anxiety attacks? This chapter holds the answers!

What Is a Panic Attack?

Panic attacks are episodes of intense fear that come on very suddenly. That fear causes a severe physical reaction. Panic attacks can occur even when there is no real danger or apparent cause for them. They may make you feel like you're losing control, having a heart attack, or even dying. They can be really scary.

We've talked in many chapters about how anxiety shows up in your body with tense muscles, sweaty palms, headaches, and stomachaches. But panic attacks take it much further than that. Panic attack symptoms are like regular anxiety symptoms on steroids.

There are two main types of panic attacks: expected and unexpected. Expected panic attacks can be tied to a specific cause or "trigger," while unexpected panic attacks occur for no specific reason. In unexpected panic attacks, your panic attack comes out of the blue.

What Causes Panic Attacks?

Expected panic attacks happen when you come into contact with something that triggers your anxiety. We've talked about triggers before, but here's a review of some common ones: family problems, excessive coffee drinking, remembering something traumatic that happened to you, and academic struggles.

Panic attacks can be frightening. Not only are they intense and severe, but they also resemble other health crises, such as heart attacks. You may not realize that you are having a panic attack. You may just think that something is very, very wrong.

Causes of frequent panic attacks may include genetics, brain chemistry, or a panic disorder. Just because you have one or two panic attacks, though, doesn't mean you have a panic disorder. It is possible to have a panic attack or two during a really stressful time and then never experience them again when the stressful situation ends. For some others, panic attacks may be more frequent.

What Are the Symptoms of a Panic Attack?

Panic attacks may show up in a number of ways.

<u>Physical Symptoms</u>

- Increased heart rate
- Feeling dizzy
- Numbness or tingling
- Sweating
- Headaches
- Nausea or vomiting
- Muscle tightness
- Chills or hot flashes
- Shortness of breath

- Chest pain
- Feeling like you're choking
- Trembling
- Fatigue

Behavioral Symptoms

- Changes in diet or sleep
- Lack of interest in activities you used to enjoy
- Staying away from family or friends
- Refusal to leave home
- Inability to relax

Mental Symptoms

- Excessive worry
- Feeling hopeless or depressed
- Fear of losing control
- A sense of terrible danger
- Fear of dying

Again, prevention is the best cure. But when prevention fails, it's important to know that you are not powerless. There is a four-step method you can employ to disrupt the onset of a panic attack and re-ground yourself.

Four-Step Calm-Down Plan

Panic attacks are scary and intense. They can feel overwhelming, but again, you are *not* powerless.

Have you ever seen those fire extinguishers in glass

cases with bold red labels reading "Break Glass in Case of Emergency"? This four-step method is just such a resource to have handy.

Mount this method in the hallways of your mind. Familiarize yourself with it and consider it a powerful tool in your mental health tool belt to bring out when the heat rises. When properly applied, it will help you douse the flames of panic and climb back into the driver's seat of your mind and body.

Step 1

Retake your body and mind's steering wheel.

Panic attacks thrive on momentum. They want your mind and body to race out of control. So employ these basic steps to kick anxiety out of the driver's seat of your body and mind.

Body: Come to a physical standstill.

1. Stand with both feet planted firmly on the ground.
2. Say to yourself, aloud or in your mind, "I am still. This moment has paused."
3. Feel gravity pulling you down, pressing your whole body onto the soles of your shoes.
4. Grind one heel side to side as if you are dousing a match. You are in this place at this time.

Mind: Observe your thoughts.

Our thoughts can fill up our minds to the point of

bursting before we know it. Sometimes it feels like we don't have enough room for them inside our heads . . . so imagine them outside!

- Have you ever looked at the clouds as they blew through the sky? Some clouds are big, some small, some dark and foreboding, while others look comfortable and soft. Imagine your thoughts the same way. Point them out in a matter-of-fact, nonjudgmental way.
- "That's an anxious thought."
- "There is a big cluster of fears over there."
- "My anxious thoughts are like storm clouds, but my hopes are like puffy clouds."
- "There are some confident thoughts on the horizon. They will get here soon."
- When you do this, you can let your thoughts continue to move and run, but they do not have to take you captive. You can observe your own train of thought without being forced along for the ride!

<u>Step 2</u>
Reset your breathing.

Do you remember the 4-7-8 breathing technique from chapter 7?

1. Inhale through your nose at a slow, steady pace for **four** seconds.

2. When you are done inhaling, hold your breath in your lungs for **seven** seconds.

3. Then exhale slowly and evenly through your mouth for **eight** seconds.

Step 3

Pick out an object of focus.

As I said earlier, panic attacks are at their worst when they gain momentum. They feed on themselves, in a way. Work against the momentum of a panic attack by paying attention to a nearby object.

Earlier, you learned to imagine noticing your thoughts. This time, you want to actually notice a physical thing. It can be any object in your line of sight as long as you devote as much mental attention to it as possible.

- Is it stationary or moving?
- What shape is it?
- What is it made of?
- Does it have a smooth or rough texture?
- What color(s) is it?
- What size is it?
- Could you fit it in your pocket? Your backpack? The trunk of a car?
- Could you lift it yourself?
- Have you ever seen one of these before?
- Does it serve a purpose or is it there for decoration?
- Do you own one of these?

- Would you want one yourself?

Panic attacks feed, in part, on the energy we give them. By diverting your mental energy onto something else, something as simple as a nearby object, you can cut off the power supply that feeds their force and intensity.

Step 4

Visualize and visit your personal paradise.

"Your personal paradise" refers to the state of mind when you are able to access or produce a peaceful environment that helps you escape stress, calm down, and regain a sense of grounding.

Your personal paradise is the place that makes you breathe deep and smile when you just so much as think of it. Perhaps you have gone there before without even meaning to or knowing how you got there.

Before you can choose to visit, though, you have to decide what your personal paradise is. The more clearly you define your personal paradise, the more clearly you can give yourself directions when you need to make a visit.

Defining Your Personal Paradise

"Your personal paradise" is called that for a reason. It is all three of those things:

- **Yours:** Your personal paradise belongs to you. Nothing, not even a panic attack, has the power to take it away from you. You may forget about it or get too distracted to look for it, but it never ceases to exist. It is a resource that is always available to you. You always have it. It is yours.

- **Personal:** Your personal paradise is unique to who you are as a person. People find relaxation and peace through different methods, practices, and things. What you envision as a peaceful environment may be different from what your friend or neighbor envisions. Neither of you is wrong; you are just different people. Each person has their own mental paradise.

- **Paradise:** Perhaps you have experienced feelings of peace in a real time and place you have actually been before, and you mentally return there. Or perhaps your paradise is somewhere you have always wanted to go. Perhaps it doesn't exist but is an imaginary ideal.

Visualizing Your Personal Paradise

Did something stand out or come to mind as you learned about this idea of your personal paradise? It may be a place you loved to visit or a mental "replay" of a time when you felt safe and happy.

If you were not able to draw upon an experience you've had or a place you have been, imagining an idealized place works just as well. When imagining, there are no rules, but a few guidelines may be helpful:

- Consider a natural place, such as a still lake reflecting the clouds, a green field, or a sandy beach and blue waves.
- If nature is not relaxing to you, choose a symbolic place that is known for or associated with peace. Consider the tranquility of a temple or the soothing nature of a spa. Pick a place that is easily recognizable to visualize and embodies the relaxation you want to obtain.

Visiting Your Personal Paradise

Once you have stopped, reset your breathing, focused on an object, and know your personal paradise, it's time to actually go there.

1. Close your eyes and imagine yourself in this place. You may be standing, sitting, or lying there. Whatever posture you are in, you feel balanced and calm. You have a grin on your face. You are nodding in a reassured, satisfied way.
2. Engage each of your senses in this place. Maybe you see an amazing sunset. Maybe you smell the salt of the ocean. Maybe you hear gentle music or the babbling of a river. Maybe you taste cold, fresh water. Maybe you feel the warmth of the sun on your skin.

- Do not simply view your personal paradise like a picture hanging on the wall. Transport yourself there as much as possible!
- The more real you can make this experience in your senses, the more effective it will be.
- Recognize that visiting your personal paradise is something you have to practice. During the exercise of visitation, you may find your anxious thoughts intruding. This is normal. Take a breath and gently pivot your mind back toward your visualization. Like anything else, the more you practice, the better you will get!

These four steps work in concert with one another to equip you with a basic, portable technique for regaining control that you can use anywhere and any time you feel panicked. By bringing yourself to a stop, resetting the rhythm of your breath, focusing on a physical object, and visualizing your personal paradise, you can cut off the power supply of panic attacks. When you retake control of your body and mind, you will recognize the power you have over your anxiety.

Afterword

Congratulations on finishing this book! Going through this material required courage and commitment. I know some of those exercises were tough. They encouraged you to really look at your life, dig into your emotions, and change what wasn't serving you well. That is hard work! You are really brave to do all of that!

The goal of this book was to share the tools that helped me overcome my anxiety. I want to tell as many teens as possible that, with the right tools, you can control your anxiety instead of letting it control you. By learning to do this now, you will save yourself so much future stress!

Isn't that exciting? Anxiety isn't a big scary beast that can't be beaten. I know sometimes, in the middle of a panic attack, it can feel like it is, but that's just not true. You can learn how to beat anxiety, and reading this book was an amazing place to start. However, it's not the place to end. You will probably always have moments in your life when anxiety will rear its ugly head, but it won't own you anymore. You will get to decide how much control it can have. You may need to go back over these tools a few times. Just like learning an instrument or trying a new sport, you have to practice your new skills to keep them sharp.

We've covered a lot of anxiety-fighting tools in this book. I wanted you to get the most value for your time, so I included ten chapters packed with over thirty-five exercises to help you stay calm when stress threatens to overwhelm you.

Most people who go through this book find a handful of tools that work really well for them, but then they forget about other tools that could be just as helpful. I am a big fan of having as many tools as possible to fight that terrible Anxiety Beast, so let's go back through some of the main things we covered in this book just in case there was something you missed or want to revisit.

And, in a few months, if you feel like you need a refresher, you can come back to this list to review the tools and see which ones you need to practice again.

We covered different ways to approach anxiety using the tools of:

- **Mindfulness:** You learned how visualization, breathing, and meditation can help you stay calm in the present moment.
- **Cognitive Behavioral Therapy:** We discussed the ten principles of CBT and how

it can help with anxiety. Maybe you decided to see a therapist who uses the CBT approach.

- **Dialectical Behavioral Therapy**: You saw that DBT is similar to CBT, but it also adds in mindfulness techniques.

Then we jumped into my favorite topic: overthinking and cognitive distortions. Yes, I know it's weird to say that I like that topic, but understanding those concepts helped me finally be able to overcome my own anxiety. I hope that you have been working on understanding your thought patterns. I hope that you are continuing with your gratitude journal. That practice brings me a lot of joy. Oh, and did you try that chair exercise yet? That's a powerful one! Go back and review it in chapter 3 if you need a refresher on finding creative ways to handle spinning or overwhelming thoughts.

How is catching your triggers going? I sure hope that you have been able to find healthy ways to deal with those common anxiety triggers like caffeine, toxic people, social media, family problems, and academics. Trigger mapping and state-shifting are ways to get your triggers under control. Those exercises are found in chapter 4 if you need a refresher on how to apply them to your life.

Time management can be tough. The tools in chapter 5 should have equipped you to make to-do lists and set goals. Don't worry if you've fallen out of those habits. Remember that we are looking for progress, not perfection. Just go back and review the chapter and try, try again.

Afterword

Each time you return to this material, you will grow and learn more. Also, it's normal that some of the exercises may work better for you than others. That's why I encourage readers to try each of them. You won't know what works for you until you try!

Organization goes hand in hand with time management. Think about the state of your bedroom, locker, and binders these days. If you haven't been able to maintain the order in those checklists, go back to that section in chapter 6 to review it again. Then notice how nice it feels when everything is in its place. I bet your parents and teachers will compliment you on it too!

Have you ever heard of spring cleaning? Basically, it means that near the end of winter or the beginning of spring, a lot of people clean out and reorganize their houses. I actually think it is wise to check in with your organizational state at the change of every season. Most people pretty naturally tend toward becoming more disorganized over time. Checking in with your organization a few times a year can be really helpful to keep you on track.

Has eating been a source of stress for you lately? If so, I hope you found a great therapist to work with. When you think back to the tools in chapter 7, which one was the most helpful for you? We talked about doing a body scan, 4-7-8 breathing, and mindful eating.

Chapter 8 was all about test anxiety, which is a major issue for most people in school. How did your most recent test go? Did you try the progressive muscle relaxation or red balloon visualization to get you through it? If so, I bet you noticed that your thinking was clearer, and you were able to do your best with less stress. Since you started addressing your test anxiety, have you seen any changes in your grades? I bet your friends are wondering what's changed. Don't be shy—these skills were meant to be shared! Once people see your anxiety getting better, they will naturally ask what you did. That can be a great opportunity for you to share this book with them. You can be a source of inspiration, encouragement, and healing in other people's lives!

How did learning about peer pressure in chapter 9 change your view of your friends? Maybe it made you even more thankful for their encouragement and support. Or perhaps it caused you to rethink some of your relationships. Peer pressure tends to be most intense in your teen years, but it can continue even into adulthood. Learning how to manage peer pressure now will make the rest of your life smoother and easier.

The last chapter is one I wish I did not have to write. It makes me sad to think of any of you having to deal with panic attacks. They can be so overwhelming and scary. But I knew it was important for you to make your four-step calm-down plan. That may end up being your most commonly used tool. How has it been working for you lately? Go back and review it. As you know, it is nearly impossible to try to learn a new skill during a panic attack! Put the work in now to learn your four-step calm-down plan so it's ready to go if a panic attack threatens to ruin your day.

Afterword

Now that you have finished this book, the next step is to keep using the different exercises you encountered here to help get rid of your anxiety once and for all. Whenever you need a little extra help, return to the exercises! Try to keep that beginner's mind and stay curious to keep learning more about how to manage your anxiety.

I'm encouraging you to practice these tools because they are what brought me freedom from my anxiety. They literally changed my life. I used to have trouble sleeping every night and felt nervous and on edge every day. Then I learned the skills in this book and my life became so much more peaceful. Once I saw the power of these tools, I just couldn't keep them to myself. I wrote this book so they can help you too.

You can also continue sharing this important, empowering message. If you want more teens with anxiety to get the help they need, please write a review of this book on Amazon. It only takes about one minute, and that would be an amazing way to let other teens know how much this book can help them. It will also help me to spread the word about this book, and I would be grateful to you!

Together we can create a world free of anxiety by sharing these tools with the world, one person at a time!

Simply by letting other people know how this book has helped you and what they'll discover as they turn the pages, you'll show them how to find the help they need.

Thank you for your help. When you know how difficult it is to live with anxiety, it's natural to want to help others in the same situation.

Pass It On!

As you continue to build your skills to manage your anxiety, you put yourself in the perfect position to help someone just like you.

Simply by leaving your honest opinion of this book on Amazon, you'll show other young people where they can find all the tools and techniques that are helping you.

Thank you so much for your support. All too many people think they have to live with their anxiety – together, we can let them know that there's a better way.

>>> Click here to leave your review on Amazon. https://tinyurl.com/tamingbeast

Made in United States
North Haven, CT
26 October 2023

43215377R00087